Praise for
Risking Church

"*Risking Church* is a bold book at a critical moment. Jim invites us to a Church that we may have never seen before. It's a place where we are safe to expose our sin to one another while looking ahead to one another's glory, where more than programs and rhetoric are used to draw us from our hiding, and where there is power sufficient to cause lasting change. And all of this not only in theory but also in practice from a pastor whose own story demonstrates even his need for this type of true community. This is required reading for any churchgoer."

—DEREK WEBB, singer and songwriter

"In a society filled with hurting people, God's people must fulfill the calling to authentically live a life of grace and truth. The church Jim Kallam describes will attract those who need Christ, because it is the church He envisioned. Jim lives that life, and his church models what Christ desires for all churches."

—WILLIAM J. HAMEL, president, Evangelical Free Church of America

"For many, church has been one of the best places to hide—from our real selves, from others, even from God. But it doesn't have to be so. In this graciously written, honestly told book, my friend Jim Kallam shows how one pastor and one church learned to live truth in community, to be set free to enjoy 'the glorious liberty of the children of God.' *Risking Church* will help you to take the risks that could change your life—and your church!"

—LEIGHTON FORD, president of Leighton Ford Ministries in Charlotte, North Carolina

"Jim Kallam, with great skill, authenticity, and biblical insight, has given a gift to the church, reminding us who we are and the way we were—and are supposed to be. This book is also a gift to old, cynical preachers like me and to you, even if you are neither old nor cynical. Read it and rejoice!"

—STEVE BROWN, author and professor at Reformed Theological Seminary in Orlando, Florida, and the Bible teacher on the syndicated radio program *Key Life*

"Jim Kallam has masterfully cast a vision for an organism that lives, loves, and struggles together—the Church as it was meant to be. I recommend this book to any whose heart yearns for authentic community, as mine does."

—JEREMY THIESSEN, musician, downhere

"Jim Kallam has a passion *and* a plan to help us stop playing church and start experiencing the real thing. As he points out, the risks are real—but they're also well worth it. *Risking Church* shows what a genuine community of grace and personal growth (rather than just numerical growth) looks, smells, and feels like. And what it takes to get there. May his tribe increase."

—LARRY OSBORNE, author of *The Unity Factor* and pastor of North Coast Church in Vista, California

"Disenchantment with church life is on the increase. Now Jim Kallam has given us an excellent guide to the restoration of church fellowship, in humility and personal transparency, that is inspiring to read. Every church member needs to read this."

—JAMES M. HOUSTON, board of governors' professor of spiritual theology, Regent College, Vancouver, Canada

Risking Church

Risking

CREATING A PLACE WHERE *Your* HEART FEELS AT HOME

Church

Jim Kallam Jr.

WATERBROOK
PRESS

RISKING CHURCH
PUBLISHED BY WATERBROOK PRESS
2375 Telstar Drive, Suite 160
Colorado Springs, Colorado 80920
A division of Random House, Inc.

All the stories in this book are true, but some names and circumstances have been changed to protect the identities of the persons involved.

ISBN 1-57856-651-7

Published in association with Yates & Yates, LLP, Attorneys and Counselors, Orange, California.

Library of Congress Cataloging-in-Publication Data
Kallam, Jim.
  Risking church : creating a place where your heart feels at home / Jim Kallam.— 1st ed.
    p. cm.
  ISBN 1-57856-651-7
  1. Church. 2. Community—Religious aspects—Christianity. I. Title.
  BV600.3.K35 2003
  253—dc22

                                    2003014605

Printed in the United States of America
2003—First Edition

10 9 8 7 6 5 4 3 2 1

To Suzi,
my beautiful bride.

———━☱◉☲━———

For twenty-eight years
you have been my constant, loving community.

One thing I know:
I've got you, Babe.

Contents

Part Four: Stories of Community

14 A Story of Hope 119
15 A Story of Growth 125
16 A Story of Restoration 135
17 A Story of Faithfulness 141

Epilogue: My Prayer for the Church 145
Notes 149
Acknowledgments 155

When a Church Becomes
a Community

I remember the moment my thinking shifted. It was two in the morning. I was sitting at the patio table in our South Florida home, working on my first book. The year was 1973.

I'd been out of graduate school three years, with a framed Ph.D. diploma in clinical psychology to show for my efforts and a government-issued private practice certificate that qualified me to charge people for talking with them.

Crumpled papers were scattered about on the patio floor, and I was sitting back in my chair, confused and frustrated. I'd been "doing therapy" for a while, people kept coming, and some seemed to improve. And I was making a living. But I sensed something wasn't right. Deeper issues were going on that I wasn't reaching.

I was already facing the impotence of psychology to do what most needed to be done in people's lives, and I was asking what a Christian worldview had to offer. What was *real* change, and how was Christianity supposed to help? My blank legal pad remained blank. I didn't know.

A TURNING POINT...AND A PROBLEM

Suddenly the proverbial light bulb went on. Looking back, it was only a fifteen-watter. But it seemed like a floodlight at the time. My mind went into high gear.

We bear the image of God. I don't know what all that means, but somehow we're like God. We're persons, like He is, and we've been designed to be whole only in community, to enjoy the kind of community the Trinity enjoys.

But we're unlike God in our dependency. We're needy. He's not. And we're sinful. We need Him first to forgive us and then to satisfy our desires to be loved and to know we matter. And we can most acutely feel secure and significant when we're in the company of people who love like Jesus and when we're making a difference in one another's lives.

"Wait a minute!" I remember standing and shouting loud enough to wake my wife. "That's the church! That's God's plan for dealing with all our personal struggles. We need community!"

That was a turning point, an early watershed in my thinking. From that point on, I've always believed that good things could happen in people's souls in a church community that could happen nowhere else, not even in a paid professional hour.

Over the last thirty years, I've run into a problem that has considerably dampened my early enthusiasm: The church rarely functions like a community. Empire-building, surface fellowship, dull Bible studies, exciting sermons that create expectations that are soon disappointed, ministry opportunities that impose burdens more than release giftedness, bickering elders who spend more time tending to business than to sheep—so many ingredients have twisted the church into the shape of an organization, a business, a corporate structure, rather than a simple community of pilgrims journeying to God.

I've struggled with disillusionment and cynicism. I've felt anger toward pastors. I've wondered why I should even bother with church. I once felt so lonely during a church service I had to get up and leave before I burst into tears.

HOPE RESTORED

Twenty years ago I met someone who has helped restore my hope for the church. A young pastor named Jim Kallam came to a counseling seminar I was leading, and we met and agreed to have dinner together. Over our meal, Jim and his wife, Suzi, shared some marital tensions they were experiencing.

I remember thinking, *These two people are real. No phony image stuff here. And they seem to think that following Christ and inviting a few others to join them on their journey might make a real difference in their lives.* I left the table that evening drawn to them both, knowing that I could sit under the teaching and pastoral leadership of a man like this. We've been close friends ever since.

When I feel cynicism creeping back into my soul regarding the church, I think of four pastors: Kent Denlinger, Trip Moore, Dwight Edwards, and Jim Kallam. Jim's special contribution has been to restore my hope that even a sizeable church can become a real community, a group of broken believers who radically depend on Christ in the ways they relate to one another.

It's happening in Church at Charlotte under Jim's leadership. No pastor I know is more gifted in creating a churchwide atmosphere of safety where people can encounter grace in the middle of honest struggle. When a church becomes a community, its relevance is deepened as it becomes *ir*relevant to wrong objectives, such as looking good, feeling comfortable with complacency, and enjoying social spirituality. That's happening in Charlotte.

BLUEPRINT FOR REVOLUTION

I believe a revolution is brewing. The Spirit is focusing our attention on the doctrine of the Trinity, and some of us are staggering under the implications of that doctrine for how we are meant to relate to one another. And as He's shining His light on what has long been in the dark—the theology of the new covenant, which tells us we already have everything we need to become a community—He's stirring our appetite to get on with it.

What we lack is a model. We have plenty of models for how to build a thriving church, how to instruct individual Christians to grow in their faith, and how to finance building programs and strengthen missions emphases.

But we don't have a clear model for how a church can become a community. We haven't thought through how people can feel safe enough in the presence of grace to stop pretending they're doing better than they are. And we haven't understood how we can relate with broken people as broken friends who together can experience deep spiritual formation.

Jim's book provides the model we need. It's a "narrative model." He teaches, he exegetes, and he tells stories, true stories from his own life as one humble, struggling, hopeful member of a community. Among his considerable gifts, what stands out to me is his wise, gentle strength in knowing how to lead a congregation of nearly fifteen hundred into an experience of meaningful connecting. No one I know does it better.

Thirty years ago, the lights went on. I saw that God's plan for healing His people centered in the church. But I saw too that to fulfill God's plan, the church needed to become a community.

Everything needed is already in place. Jim's wisdom lights the path to releasing the church to become a community—not programming it or organizing it to become what it's not, but releasing the church to reveal what it already is: a community of people who are called to struggle well together under the authority of the Bible, in the power of the Spirit, longing to know Christ better, for the glory of the Father.

This book could provide the blueprint for the coming revolution.

—DR. LARRY CRABB

To Know and Be Known

Starbucks recently opened a coffee shop near my office. It has become a place of retreat for me, a place to sit, think, and observe people.

You learn a lot about people by just sitting and watching. Most folks rush in and out each morning to get to work or to an appointment on time. Others come in, order their latte or cappuccino, find a table, and begin a conversation with friends.

Many of us are regular customers; we know the names of the folks who work there. We exchange greetings, call each other by name, and ask how the other person is doing. The coffee shop is a place where people know each other, where lives intersect.

The interactions are surface, I know that; but something about this scene draws me. I can sense an underlying and more central reality about life—we all want to know and be known by others. We want to be able to relate as real persons, to share our lives, our hopes and fears, and to reveal what makes us unique creations of God. That's community.

I pastor a church just down the road from Starbucks. I've been there a long time, more than twenty-seven years. With the smell of coffee arousing my imagination, I long for our church to become a community. I want everything I see at the coffee shop and so much more. I want us to be a community where programs aren't nearly as important as the journey we share together. *I want life in the church to be important.*

I recently met with a young man in his twenties who had just begun attending our church. As we talked, he said something that still haunts me: "I'm always inviting friends to come to church with me," he said, "but people my age don't want to go to church." I asked him why that was. He sat quietly before responding, then offered, "They just don't think it's important." Doctors are important. Working to get a paycheck is important. The weekly appointment with a therapist is important. Feeling good about ourselves is important. Having fun is important. But involvement in church just isn't that important.

TRACED TO GOD'S HEART

From all directions, the church takes its shots. The world sees us as hypocrites, irrelevant to real life. Insiders look around and criticize because something wasn't done the right way; our "needs" were not met.

Let's face it: The church is flawed and many times leaves people disappointed. The criticisms are too often warranted. And that really isn't hard to understand because the church is made up of people like you and me—flawed people, people who make mistakes, who disappoint others and who many times just don't get it right. It's true. Headlines thunder about another Christian leader's moral failure. We hear the quiet rustle as another disillusioned person slips out the back door, never to return.

Sometimes I want to cry—sometimes I do cry. It can be so discouraging. I can easily relate when the author of Hebrews says, "Therefore, strengthen your feeble arms and weak knees."[1] I need that kind of encouragement. (I suspect you do too.) I need to know that, with all its shortcomings, *the church has a purpose and possibility that can be traced to the very heart of God.*

In his Chronicles of Narnia, C. S. Lewis paints a picture of a land in real need of encouragement. The land is Narnia. The evil witch is in control. It's always winter, but never Christmas. Characters in the story—the Beavers and the children Peter, Lucy, and Susan—are skulking through the land, seeking to avoid the witch. One morning they awake to the sound of bells. Worried that it's the witch's sleigh, they send Mr. Beaver out from the cave to investigate. He calls them out and, as they risk a peek, they find themselves face to face with a huge man in a bright red, fur-lined robe. His great white beard flows down to his chest. It's Father Christmas. "I have come at last," he says. "She has kept me out for a long time, but I got in at last. *Aslan is on the move.*" Aslan, of course, is the lion—the figure of Christ.

I need the encouragement that Christ is on the move. I need to know God is up to something in my life and in the life of the church, something important, something so important that nobody will want to miss it.

Hebrews says, "In these last days [God] has spoken to us by his Son."[2] Speech means action. God is active in our lives, working through Jesus. From the time He shouted in joy over His Son coming up out of the waters of baptism until now, God has funneled all that He wants for you and me through Jesus.

Dietrich Bonhoeffer, in the last days before his execution, expressed the reality that Christ is on the move. Bonhoeffer lived and died with an encouragement that found its source not in the circumstances of his life, but in the person of Jesus Christ:

The key to everything is the "in him." All that we may rightly expect from God, and ask him for, is to be found in Jesus Christ.... If we are to learn what God promises, and what he fulfills, we must persevere in quiet meditation on the life, sayings, deeds, sufferings and death of Jesus.[3]

I Have a Vision

Through His Son, Jesus, God has made it possible for His people to be a community like no other. He wants us to consider each other more important than the Rotary, Kiwanis, or any other service club. God is calling us to be a true community—a life-giving, life-sharing, life-revealing community that's available only to the followers of Jesus.

I have a vision for community, and I want to explore that vision in these pages. Church can once again become important. It will happen only when we learn to relate to one another in a new way, a living way, so that we become a *living* church.

I long for this to happen in the church I pastor. It has already begun, but I want more. And I long for it to happen in the church you attend. We can become the living church, a place where love is actively expressed, where we arouse in one another a deepening love for God and for each other. In spite of the church's flaws and weaknesses, it *is* possible. The church can be released to become a community. Why? Because God has spoken through His Son. *Aslan is on the move!*

PART ONE

Where Community Begins

Why Am I Still a Pastor?

When the world sees a church from which selfishness is banished,
then it will acknowledge the divine mission of Christ because he has
wrought such a wonder, a community of men who truly and
heartily love one another.

ANDREW MURRAY

This has been a lousy week! Two couples I know are separating. Two young girls are battling for their lives with cancer. (I really hate that word.) An elderly man with much to live for lies in a nursing-home bed, giving up on life. I've received e-mails from friends about parents dying and jobs being lost. In the language of the day—life sucks! That sounds crude, but it describes how many feel. Solomon used nicer words, still with equal force:

> "Meaningless! Meaningless!"
> says the Teacher.

"Utterly meaningless!

Everything is meaningless."[1]

Everything from wisdom and study to seeking pleasure and pursuing work; from advancing in power and prestige to achieving wealth—it's all meaningless! It isn't easy to make sense of life.

Like I said, it's been a lousy week.

If this week's events were isolated occurrences, I could philosophize and believe hope is just around the corner. There's just one problem: They are not isolated. Weeks like this are repeated over and over again in my own life and in the life of our congregation. Similar stories are found in communities all around this country. They're found in your community.

As I sat by myself the other week at a bagel shop, I found myself staring out the window at a young man mowing the grass. All of a sudden I felt a strong urge to run out, grab the mower, and take over his job. My mind raced: *I don't want to be a pastor anymore. I want to cut grass for a living.* What produced that kind of thinking? Was it a random thought, or was it a lasting change of heart?

As I sat and reflected, I began to understand the appeal of cutting grass. When you're finished, the job is complete. The end result is a beautiful, neat lawn and a sense of order. A freshly cut lawn stands in sharp contrast to the uncertainty and chaos in people's lives—and in my own.

DOES IT MATTER?

Down through the years, the idealism with which I began ministry has been chipped away by the harsh realities of ministry life. In 1981 I was ordained. I wrote my thesis, studied what I believe, and was ready to be examined. I survived several hours of being grilled by men whose sole job was to examine my beliefs and make me feel very uncomfortable. They did their job with flying colors; somehow I passed.

My ordination service was a joyous occasion of confirmation, followed by a celebration. I stood in line receiving congratulations while holding our three-year-old daughter, Kelly, in my arms. One gentleman who spoke to me turned next to Kelly and asked, "Do you know what today is?" She nodded, looked him in the eyes, and said, "Today is the day they make my daddy king!" Oh, from the mouths of babes.

The years since haven't left me feeling very kingly. The journey has produced a variety of emotions and countless questions. Questions of what God was doing. Questions of whether what I was doing mattered. Questions that, at times, even called my faith into doubt.

All these years later, however, I'm still a pastor. I believe that twenty years from now I'll still be a pastor. Why?

In some ways the answer is simple; in other ways, complicated. The simple answer: God has called me to serve Him in this way. The more complicated answer is found in the many defining moments that have shaped my call, some of which I'll reveal in the coming pages. I'm certain more defining times will mark the journey ahead. There are, however, two fundamental truths that frame the answer to my many questions.

Two Framing Truths

The first truth declares the location of my confidence in life.

> Such confidence as this is ours through Christ before God.
> Not that we are competent in ourselves to claim anything

for ourselves, but our competence comes from God. He has
made us competent as ministers of a new covenant—not of
the letter but of the Spirit; for the letter kills, but the Spirit
gives life.[2]

My confidence is in Christ, not in any performance or answers I may
offer. I'm a recipient of a new covenant relationship with God. Jesus died
for me and for you. In doing so He accomplished something we could
never earn—forgiveness of our sin. When I put my faith in this truth, His
Spirit began living in me. Because of this new covenant and the Spirit's
presence, we "find ourselves qualified by God to live as God intends us to
live today."[3]

This confidence affects the way I live. It's seen in everyday choices. It
surfaces in major decisions and in the countless uncertainties I face. And it
shapes my understanding of what I have to offer others. Christ living in me
gives me the capability to impact others.

The second truth is that the church is vital in my growth and journey
with Christ. What is vital about the church isn't found in any programs or
services. It's found only when the church is released to become a community, when we uncover the awesome reality that we have something to offer
one another, so much more than a smile and a quick "Hello, how are you?"

Let me illustrate the meaning of the word *release,* which is crucial to
our understanding of what makes community effective. In the springtime
I think of horse racing. If you follow the sport at all, you know there are
three important races: the Preakness, the Belmont, and the big daddy of
them all, the Kentucky Derby. These events are all about the horses: powerful, beautiful, and (hopefully) fast. These three-year-olds are ready to do
one thing—run. They are built for speed. But all that power is held back

by the starting gate, a simple piece of metal. Until the gate is opened, the purpose of these animals won't be realized. In fact, if the gate were never opened, you could put a mule beside a thoroughbred, and it would be equally as effective. However, when the starting gate opens, all of that power, grace, and speed explode, leaving no doubt as to the purpose of these spectacular animals.

Just so, as the life of Christ is released in each of us, and we pour His energy into one another's lives, something amazing happens. The fragrance of Jesus is experienced in our lives and in the life of our community. Problems and struggles don't vanish, but hope lights the way.

NOT BEYOND HOPE

Several years ago, a certain woman and her children began attending our church. The pain she felt over her husband's absence was deep. He wasn't simply staying home; he had left her—a sad story repeated too many times in too many communities.

Folks from our church family showed love to her and the kids. She began to experience Christ being poured into her life. The fragrance of Christ was released like a sweet-smelling perfume.

Meanwhile, two men in our church began to reach out and care for the husband. After some time, he began to attend the second of our two worship services by himself. Eventually he came back home. Their marriage is restored, and their relationship with Christ is growing.

Recently the husband shared with me that if it hadn't been for the love he felt from this community, and in particular from those two men, he doubted if he would ever have come back. It wasn't what he'd expected from a church. "I thought I would be judged and pushed aside, but people really loved me. Sam and Eric in particular offered me hope. Despite all I'd done and all my failures, they demonstrated that my life wasn't beyond hope. God could rebuild my marriage and my life."

Why am I still a pastor? What keeps me going in the mess that we call life? Two things: First, I believe in what Christ has done and made possible. Second, I believe in the church. Communities of people who walk together and believe that God can use them to stir one another to long even more deeply for Christ—that's the church.

A Better Way

The first priority—the foundation for community with others and personal transformation—is an encounter with God. The new way makes that possible. It makes a way for us to draw near to God.

LARRY CRABB

The whole dispensation of the Spirit, the whole economy of grace in Christ Jesus, the whole of our spiritual life, the whole of the health and growth and strength of the church has been laid down and provided for and secured in the New Covenant.

ANDREW MURRAY

I don't need your help, I can do it myself!" That's the proud cry of freedom spoken by every child in the process of growing up. I still feel good when I remember walking to school alone, without Mom or Dad by my side. Then came the day I actually rode my bike to Golden's 5 & 10 in the next town. And finally—the ultimate rite of passage—I received my driver's license and drove a car with no adult on board.

Every child longs for freedom and misdefines it as independence. We're taught that hard work and education can accomplish anything. Americans prize that way of thinking, for this is the land of the individual and individual rights. We can make it happen. It's the western way, taught and modeled with powerful consistency.

Being unable to do something is unthinkable, unacceptable. We love to believe we can overcome the most challenging obstacles. A spaceship that can carry a man to the moon? Been there, done that. Surgery that removes a diseased organ and replaces it with a healthy one? It happens every week in hospitals all over the country. And now we've charted the DNA code of the human body. What's next? Bring on new challenges. We'll handle them—we can do it.

At times, however, we face an obstacle too difficult to conquer.

THE DREADED ROPE

Growing up, I was a good athlete. I loved every sport and could play most without fear of embarrassing myself. But one challenge proved too great. Essex Fells Elementary School required an annual fitness evaluation, which involved running, jumping, sit-ups, and the dreaded rope climb. The rope hung from the girder like a long, limp snake: I was supposed to climb it. I still flush when I remember my buddies standing in a group, laughing at my repeated failed attempts. No matter how hard I tried, I couldn't get my tall, skinny body up that rope. On evaluation day, I begged my parents to let me stay home. More than once, I feigned sickness to avoid The Rope.

Those days, thankfully, are behind me, but I still encounter challenges today that I cannot overcome. And the consequences of adult failure are far worse, I'm discovering, than mere embarrassment.

My journey in ministry spans twenty-seven years, all in one city and all at one church. In many ways, however, my exposure to and understanding of ministry began years before. I grew up in a home where both Dad and Mom were involved in ministry. I learned early that the world of ministry could be even more daunting than The Rope. It was a world based on external standards that needed to be "climbed." When you performed well, you were pronounced acceptable. When you didn't, people said you were backslidden and added your name to the prayer list. I learned at an early age how to play the game, and I played it very well. I wasn't going to end up on someone's prayer list.

Two incidents clearly typified for me this external performance-based mentality.

On the far end of our church's parking lot sat a Howard Johnson's restaurant. A few buddies and I loved to sneak over there at the break between Sunday school and the worship service, sometimes even during Sunday school. One Sunday, I was coming back across the parking lot eating a PayDay candy bar (still a favorite of mine) when, out of no-where, one of the deacons materialized. He grabbed my arm and gruffly announced that we were going to find my parents. I wasn't certain what my crime was, but I knew it must be a felony. My confusion increased as he smugly told my dad that he'd caught me smoking. Then he added, "No one who calls himself a Christian would ever smoke." My father's sense of fairness saved the day, as he soon discovered that PayDays come in white wrappers.

Several years later, at age sixteen, I decided to join the church. One of the requirements was to share my testimony in front of the deacons. Our church had a room off the lobby called the Deacons' Room. I was ushered into that room and took my seat at the end of a long mahogany table lined with the faces of white-haired balding men. They listened for a while, excused me, and after several agonizing minutes finally brought me back in to hear their verdict. By an act of mercy, I passed and was welcomed into membership.

While that fact was sinking in, they slid a piece of paper and a pen across the table toward me. They informed me that this was a covenant that, as a member, I must sign and agree to keep. As my eyes drifted down the page, the phrase *Thou shalt not...* kept jumping out. I was not to attend movies, play cards, drink alcohol, dance, or smoke anything—whether I inhaled or not. I had many questions, but the eyes staring at me made it clear that I was not to question but merely to sign.

MY SHAKEN WORLD

Though at times I fought against this approach to the Christian life and ministry, the legalistic mind-set was already deeply instilled. As I entered the ministry, I assumed—and therefore communicated—that performing well brought more love from God. Doing good made you more acceptable and kept you off prayer lists.

Although I would have vigorously denied it, that belief drove me as I pastored. I pleased God more by being a youth pastor than I ever could have by playing professional baseball. That's how I thought, even though baseball was what I loved.

It wasn't until 1990, fourteen years into my ministry, that God shook my world enough to let me see that I'd been seduced. The challenge came during a brief sabbatical when, through the Holy Spirit using a friend as a spiritual director and a book by Steve Brown, *When Being Good Isn't Good Enough,* I saw something I hadn't seen before. The apostle Paul's words to the Galatians exposed my wrongheadedness:

> You foolish Galatians! Who has bewitched you?… Did you receive the Spirit by observing the law, or by believing what you heard? Are you so foolish? After beginning with the Spirit, are you now trying to attain your goal by human effort?… Does God give you his Spirit and work miracles among you because you observe the law, or because you believe what you heard?[1]

The gospel is great news! God's grace is rich and free! For the first time in my life, the gospel took me beyond the beginning of my journey. It became for me what God always intended it to be—the core of an ongoing relationship. In my earlier thinking, the gospel had been about that initial time when I "accepted" Jesus as Savior—and it stopped there. Grace, so essential in our entering a relationship with God, somehow faded from view; I had assumed that after being saved by grace, we Christians were expected to perform, to observe the law.

During my sabbatical, I saw that the gospel at its core is a lifelong reality. God did something for me that I could never accomplish without Him when He gave me a secure relationship with Him and called me to live a "better way." I'm discovering what that way is.

RADICALLY NEW

The writer to the Hebrews was convinced not only that God had spoken (taken action) through His Son, but that the action of Jesus provided the means to live a radically new life:

> Therefore, brothers, since we have confidence to enter the Most Holy Place by the blood of Jesus, by a new and living way opened for us through the curtain, that is, his body, and since we have a great priest over the house of God, let us draw near to God with a sincere heart in full assurance of faith, having our hearts sprinkled to cleanse us from a guilty conscience and having our bodies washed with pure water. Let us hold unswervingly to the hope we profess, for he who promised is faithful. And let us consider how we may spur one another on toward love and good deeds. Let us not give up meeting together, as some are in the habit of doing, but let us encourage one another—and all the more as you see the Day approaching.[2]

God did something radical. He provided us with a new way to live through a new arrangement, what the Bible calls the new covenant. He has given us what we could never give ourselves—forgiveness of sins and a relationship with Him. His gift places before us three distinct challenges: (1) drawing near to God, (2) holding fast to our hope, and (3) spurring one another on to lives of love, good deeds, and mutual encouragement.

Before Christ, all this was unavailable. You simply couldn't live life this way. Jesus has given us something new! Through His life, death, and resurrection, He opened a new way, a way never before available to anyone or lived by anyone, something previously unattainable.

It moves us far beyond what the law made possible. It's a better way.

NOT TELLING THEM HOW TO LIVE

I long for the community I pastor to understand and live this better way. I grew up in an old covenant church, where old covenant sermons were preached and old covenant lifestyles were applauded and prized. "Do this and you will live. You'll be applauded by people and blessed by God." That's the old way, an understanding of life rooted in a covenant that has been replaced.

For years I carried old covenant thinking into my ministry. I used tools like guilt and pressure to produce change, but they produced only boiling anger in me and growing frustration in the people. A friend wisely but firmly offered this direction: "You're an angry man, with no passion beyond control. I wouldn't cross the street to hear you preach." I sat stunned. As his words sank in, I realized they were true.

That has changed.

Several years later, a couple who had been a part of our ministry for years came to tell me they were leaving our church. To personally come and tell me was unusual—most folks just turn and leave. Over lunch I asked, "Why?"

"You've changed," they said. "You're no longer telling us how to live."

As they continued to talk and share their concerns, I remember feeling a settled peace internally. Their concerns represented a problem to them— and growth to me. My job, I had learned, was less telling people what to do and more releasing them to follow their deepest desires. God can be approached by this new and living way, the way of the Spirit, because of the realities of the new covenant.

FOUR CORE REALITIES

Jesus was always butting heads with the mainline religious people of His day. Why? He taught a new way to live. Hundreds of years before Jesus came, God spoke of this new and living way through His prophet Ezekiel. He spoke of a coming day that would radically alter people's relationships with Him:

> I will sprinkle clean water on you, and you will be clean; I will cleanse you from all your impurities and from all your idols. I will give you a new heart and put a new spirit in you; I will remove from you your heart of stone and give you a heart of flesh.… You will be my people, and I will be your God.[3]

We can identify four core realities in this new and living way. They form the foundation for our lives and for releasing the church to become a community. These core realities are present in every follower of Jesus Christ.[4]

What's true in my life is true in yours. First, God has given me a *new purity.* He has taken *all* the filth and ugliness of my sin and has cleansed me. What amazes me is that this includes all the unseen things in my life—my thoughts, my motives, and every time I hide from others and from myself. Old covenant living focused on the externals: The outside was washed and cleaned, but the internal was left untouched. In the new covenant, it's *all* washed clean by the blood of Christ. As a result, I stand pure before God. It has nothing to do with me and everything to do with Jesus.

Second, God has given me a *new identity*. He has adopted me into the family. I'm His child, no longer a stranger or an enemy—I belong to Him.

One of my great joys is my family. There are certain things I enjoy because my last name is Kallam. The same is true for those who know Christ—we're family. My eternal name is Christian.

Third, I've been given a *new inclination*. The writer of Ezekiel calls it a "new heart." The author of Hebrews declares we have had our "hearts sprinkled to cleanse us," and God's law has been placed in our hearts.[5] It's a new desire to move toward Him, for I now have an urge to choose the things that are pleasing to God. At my core, I'm a forgiven child of God whose heart is inclined toward Him. That means when my wife and I are angry with each other and I feel unkind things toward her, there's actually something more central than anger that stirs in me toward Suzi. I have the capacity to love her because I have experienced Christ's love for me.

Fourth, He has given me a *new power*. The Holy Spirit living within me is the power source for this new life. This new and living way is a supernatural lifestyle made possible by God's Spirit.

Without this new purity, new identity, new inclination, and new power, my entire life is a long, dreaded rope that's impossible to climb.

Jesus has made possible a better way. "Jesus has become the guarantee of a better covenant."[6]

True for Churches

I'm beginning to grasp the way we're designed to live. We can stir one another to new covenant living based upon the realities each of us possesses through Christ.

What excites me as a pastor is that this is true not only for individuals and small groups but also for each of our churches. Think about the possibilities! People encouraging one another to live not on the basis of performance demands but on spiritual provisions; people living in an environment that will stir them in their everyday lives and release them to live in ways that bring glory to God; an entire church functioning in miraculous ways because of the provision of the Spirit through the new covenant.

I have a vision for the church. And it begins with creating an atmosphere, an environment where supernatural living is encouraged.

Like Fish to Water

Christianity means community through Jesus Christ and in Jesus Christ. No Christian community is more or less than this. Whether it be a brief, single encounter or the daily fellowship of years, Christian community is only this. We belong to one another only through and in Jesus Christ.

DIETRICH BONHOEFFER

Ten years ago I was introduced to the underwater world of snorkeling. That world amazed me then and still does. As my masked face penetrates the surface of the ocean, I'm drawn into a new world of vivid color, unevenly shaped coral, and an endless variety of squiggly organisms that thrive in that soundless space.

It's impossible to describe the beauty of that world to someone who has never been there. Underwater disposable cameras cannot tell the story. When I display my pictures, I quickly apologize—they don't portray the wonders I've seen. The thought has crossed my mind, *If I could grab the fish and remove the coral and bring them home, my friends would be able to experience the beauty I've seen.* But I can't. The fish and coral would die. God created these beautiful creatures to live in a certain environment. Leave them there and they flourish; remove them and they die.

The same is true for us. The beauty of redeemed humanity is most visible in a certain environment. God designed us to live and thrive and reflect His beauty in community. We're built for community—a supernatural environment that flows out of the living reality of Christ and what He has accomplished for us and placed in us. As surely as fish must live in water, so people must live in community.

RUNNING DEEP

When we read that God said, "Let us make man in our image, in our likeness,"[1] we often reduce the definition of that likeness to man's ability to choose, to think, to emote—all of which are true. But likeness and image have more depth. God is a relational being. He exists in one essence, yet in three persons. This relationship between Father, Son, and Spirit has existed for all eternity, and the mark of that image is built into the fabric of our being:

> The life of God-the-Trinity has planted in our souls a
> hunger for community.... Rooted, and at home with our
> desire, we are free—within the love of the Trinity—to give
> ourselves generously to others. This is to be the defining
> characteristic of the church.[2]

In that community, God has called us to live a life of love and encouragement. The author of Hebrews invites us to "consider" something:

And let us consider how we may spur one another on
toward love and good deeds. Let us not give up meeting
together, as some are in the habit of doing, but let us
encourage one another—and all the more as you see the
Day approaching.[3]

We pay lip service to the truth that we can love and encourage one
another that deeply, but most of us don't experience it. Church doesn't
make the short list in our lives.

That word *consider* in the Hebrews passage means "to pay close attention to, to look closely at." That command calls us to focus our thoughts
and attention on something, to enter a new world and see something special. But what is it?

The church too often focuses on the wrong things. I learned early on
in ministry that success boils down to three things, the ABCs of ministry:
Attendance, Buildings, and Cash. If all three are in place, your church will
be viewed as a success. In that view, the church isn't much different from
the business world, and what it takes to be a "good" pastor is frighteningly
similar to what's required to be a good CEO.

Many years ago my wife and I were overnight guests in the home of an
acquaintance. He was hosting a party, and twenty or so people had gath-
ered for a fun evening. We knew only our host, so the time dragged on with
polite, social chitchat. As we were getting ready to excuse ourselves for the
night, the conversation shifted to a friend of theirs who was overseas. They
told stories about him and laughed about the past.

Then the suggestion was made to call him. Someone else quickly
pointed out that it was 3 A.M. in that country, but they made the call
anyway.

They were well into passing the phone around and laughing when Suzi and I excused ourselves and went to bed. When we were alone, I could no longer hold back the tears. I didn't know these people. Why was I crying? I'm built for community. At that time in my life I hadn't experienced much of it. The longing for it, however, ran deep, and being on the fringe of experiencing it left me wanting more.

Removing fish from water isn't a good idea. It kills the fish. Failing to create the environment Christians need to flourish has an almost equally lethal effect. When our focus is wrong in the following areas, our lives will never reflect God's beauty as richly as they could otherwise.

ORGANIZATIONS OVER ORGANISM

First, too many churches focus more on the organization than on the organism.

Of course, the church is both organization and organism, but in many cases organization gains top billing. I remember sitting in a worship service several years ago when my mind drifted to the fact that the next evening the elders would gather for our monthly meeting. I mentally ran through our agenda—staff positions to be filled, a building campaign to be discussed, the issue of new computers.

When I went to the pulpit to speak, I looked out at the congregation. There was Pete who had just lost his job, and Mary and John who had recently gotten married. Another family was struggling with their teenage daughter, anguish written all over their faces. Where were they on our agenda? Under "other items as time allows." They each needed a community where love and encouragement could be given and received. In the struggle of life, God has called us to enter not only into our own lives but also into the lives of others.

Today things are changing in our church. We're not where we need to be, but we're moving in the right direction. If you were to sit in an elders' meeting today, you would find the majority of our time is spent on people and how to help folks we love experience the life-changing reality of Jesus.

ACCOMPLISHMENTS OVER ATMOSPHERE

Second, too many churches prize accomplishments more than creating an atmosphere.

Most pastors' conferences draw attendees with the promise that they'll learn how to do it, grow it, and duplicate it. Certain pastors and churches are lifted up as models of success. For what? Genuine community? No, for impressive accomplishments, usually centering on numbers. We think that if we listen to the experts and put into practice what they've done, their plan can work for us. We want ministry to be explained in terms that allow us to function as technicians, managers, or building contractors. We want a blueprint to build from and a list to check off as we accomplish each item.

I want something different. I want the leadership of our church to be about creating an atmosphere, an environment where people can fall in love with Jesus. I don't want technicians who can run a program. I want agents of love who will spread the life of the Spirit throughout the church.

This desire drives my engineers and accountants nuts! They want plans; I want an atmosphere, an environment, a community where people can live a new way. Fish can't swim in the desert of programs. I want living water to create an ocean where beauty thrives.

Eleven years ago we made this shift in our ministry. Over lunch, one of the elders wanted to know what I envisioned for Church at Charlotte. Three thoughts popped into my mind.

I told him that I wanted Church at Charlotte to be a place where...

• people are stirred by the study of God's Word.

• people struggle well with life.

• people serve others.

It stuck. Eleven years later, I don't know what accomplishments people remember about our church, but they know the kind of community we are. They know the atmosphere we envision and the kind of soul-nourishing environment they'll find in our fellowship.

Recently a woman visited our Sunday worship service. She came with a friend, a member of our church with a heart for evangelism who had already shared the gospel with her. As the service began, she was already weeping. All through the music and then during my message, she wept. When the service ended, the visitor didn't move. Through tear-filled eyes, she pointed to the cover of the bulletin and asked her friend, "Is this really possible? If I came here would I find this to be true?" She was pointing to the phrase, *a people who struggle well with life.*

SYSTEMS OVER SHEPHERDING

Third, too many churches look to build systems more enthusiastically than they seek to shepherd people.

As I recall growing up in the church during the '60s and '70s, one thing that stands out in my memory is the phrase *transferable concepts.* To many, discipleship became a series of books to work through, each one filled with principles to be learned that would help you manage your life.

The Christian life became a project, a system. The unspoken message was this: Life can be managed if you'll take these "seven principles" and apply them to your life. Shepherding a community, on the other hand, might not seem as efficient as the systems approach, but it follows Jesus' example.

There's a problem with this approach, a rather big one. Life is unmanageable. Shepherding is messy business. It involves caring for, feeding, binding wounds, protecting, leading, and so much more. To further complicate matters, some sheep don't want guidance or help.

To avoid this mess and keep things orderly, the church in America has gravitated to systems built on principles that can be packaged and managed. As Eugene Peterson says, "We have traded in the vocation of handcrafting saints for the business of mass-producing sheep." It's certainly easier, but it lands us far from the heart of God.

God Enters the Mess

Have you ever noticed the times in Scripture when God is moved to enter into the mess of life?

In Exodus, Moses stood before a bush that mysteriously caught fire. A familiar story. But something more dramatic happened: God called Moses into service. Why? Listen to God speaking to Moses: "I have indeed seen the misery of my people.... So I have come down to rescue them."[4] In that expression, I see God's heart.

God came down to enter into the lives of His people. Why? Their lives were a mess—four hundred years of slavery with no hope of change. The heart of God was stirred. He got involved.

Another such intervention occurred at the darkest moment in Jerusalem's history. The city had fallen to Nebuchadnezzar, and three thousand people, including a young Jew named Ezekiel, had been exiled to Babylon. God spoke to Ezekiel: He was angry with the shepherds of Israel. He was against them for selfishly taking care of themselves at the expense of the people. They had allowed their congregation to wander and fall prey to vandals and corrupters. They had left the people injured and sick. People weren't receiving care in community.

Again God entered the mess of life. Why? To shepherd His people. "For this is what the Sovereign LORD says: I myself will search for my sheep and look after them. As a shepherd looks after his scattered flock when he is with them, so will I look after my sheep."[5]

The most profound instance of God's entering our world is recorded in John's gospel. "And the Word became flesh, and dwelt among us."[6] Peterson puts it this way in *The Message:* "The Word became flesh and blood, and moved into the neighborhood."[7] God saw the mess we had made, and He entered that mess to give us life. That's the heart of God. It always has been and it always will be. If we have His heart, we'll be filled with passion to stir our own lives and the lives of others to love and live better. We'll want to build community, a community of shepherds. Shepherds involve themselves in the lives of others to arouse a passion for Jesus. The result is mutual encouragement.

LEFT WITH TENSION

Fish need water. People need community. We must journey together. James Houston defines discipleship as the mystery of two people walking together. He goes on to say: "There is no such thing as *my* maturity; it is always *our* maturity."[8]

What should be vital in church life has become incidental. Consequently, people are dying in their spiritual walk because they're living outside the environment in which God designed them to live.

There's no such thing as a self-made Christian, and there's no such thing as a self-maintained Christian. You can't encourage someone in isolation, nor can you show care and concern in isolation. And you certainly can't arouse someone to love and good deeds in isolation.

We're left with a tension—an organization we call the church that, for many, is less than compelling and an environment called community that we need desperately. If we can't release churches to become communities, our spiritual growth is at risk. We'll become fish out of water; we'll be creatures made for water, dying in the desert.

TEN MEN

As I close this chapter, let me introduce you to ten guys from our church who, for the past four years, have become community to one another—and to me.

Our group began when I invited these men to join me for a six-week study. In the beginning, I was the only one who knew each of them. Mark, Mike, Jeff, Dave, Doug, Mark, Dick, Gary, Dave, and Ed are no different from most folks in your church. Wednesday mornings at seven, we meet on the fifteenth floor of a downtown Charlotte office building as a community of brothers where titles and success don't matter, though each one works hard and enjoys a measure of business success.

We come together as men who struggle as husbands, dads, and friends. We consider what it means to be followers of Jesus and what the gospel means in our everyday worlds. We swim in the environment of community and long to arouse in one another a passion to love and to live better.

We stir a fervent love for Jesus in one another. We've seen walls and barriers broken down as struggles are honestly faced. We've seen Jesus become a little more real in each of our lives.

It happens every Wednesday morning. It's an amazing experience that has become important to every man. I've watched guys show up at 6:59 who have been traveling all night on a red-eye flight just to be there. Church is being released and is becoming community for this group of men.

I'm starting to catch that aroma of community throughout our congregation. We have a long way to go. We always will. Still, an environment is developing, and hope is building. The beauty of spiritual life is becoming evident. Our church is slowly transforming itself into a community, and that makes it important to more and more people.

PART TWO

Why We Want and Need Community

4

Safety

*It is our life, shared with the lives of others, that creates the webs
that form the mystery of community.*

One day in the fall of 1998, I was having breakfast with a good friend. Later that morning we were scheduled to address a roomful of church people about the impact of the new covenant, and my assignment was to speak about the church. My friend's question at breakfast was simple: "What do you think the church should look like?" As I thought about my response, he added: "What do you want *your* church to look like?"

During the course of our breakfast conversation, we fleshed out four words—*safety, vision, wisdom,* and *power*—to describe what a church, a spiritual community, ought to possess. Those words became the basis not only for what I said later that day but also for what, to this day, I deeply believe the church should be. Later that morning, I put it this way to my audience: "I want the church to be a safe place where we envision what His Spirit is up to in our lives and discover the wisdom to release the power to move us from where we are to where we could be."

Over the months and years that have followed, that statement has been thought through, prayed over, and refined. It's now regularly presented as my vision for our church, for it represents the truth of what we can be to one another when the church is released to become a community.

The church is to be a community, a *safe* place that provides a *vision* for people and a *wisdom* for living life. It's to be a place that allows *power* to be released, enabling believers to struggle well with life.

The core words haven't changed. As a church is released to become a community, an atmosphere develops of safety, vision, wisdom, and power. Most pastors, I think, would nod in agreement, but many might mean something by these words that's quite different from what I have in mind. There's a traditional way to define and understand these four pivotal words, and then there's a new way—a way as old (and as ever-new) as the Bible.

SAFETY MATTERS

In a church, what does safety mean? What is a safe church? Where does the safety come from?

Many leaders would answer, "Doctrinal purity." The postmodern revolution gives new importance to insisting on truth. But in today's emerging culture whose themes include preference ("I have my truth, you have yours") and subjective morality ("If it feels good, it must be right"), safety often means the freedom to be you. Who you are *is* the truth. Our response to this thinking in many evangelical churches is to more strongly insist on teaching objective truth from Scripture.

For many, predictability is a factor in creating safety. Our church facility doesn't look a whole lot like a church. Our Tudor-style buildings have been mistaken for a Steak-n-Ale restaurant, an office building, even a tennis club. For years we were known as "the little church that sits back in the woods." A long drive cuts through the woods and emerges at the front of our building. A member once placed signs along the drive to explain our ministries. The series of five or six signs, one right after another, reminded me of the old Burma Shave billboard campaign. The last sign identified a ministry we, like many other churches, have called AWANA (a children's ministry that focuses on Bible memorization). The sign read: AWANA SPOKEN HERE. After reading this sign as they drove into our parking lot, one set of parent visitors nervously held on to their children, ready to split if crazy babbling broke out. Safety for them meant the promise that nothing weird would happen in our church.

Safety is sometimes measured by control. I want to control my world, and when I think I'm pulling it off, I feel safe. For many, the church's role is to define the path I can walk so I can make life work and be safe. Whether through doctrinal purity or varying approaches to truth, through control or predictability, experiencing safety matters to people.

FREE TO BE REAL

Doctrinal orthodoxy is of course vital, but it falls short of the fullness—and the true safety—that the new covenant brings to the church. Churches can offer correct doctrine yet never stimulate community. When people walk into a theologically "safe" church Sunday after Sunday but remain unknown and untouched, the church will remain unimportant in their lives.

The safety of a new covenant community brings freedom—freedom that flows out of the radical new relationship I have with Christ and that releases me to stir or impact others with whom I'm involved.

This freedom has two components: (1) the ability to be real, and (2) the awareness that someone is *for* me.

If you surveyed faithful church attendees and asked them, "True or false? I'm not the person I want to be," most would answer, "True." Then ask them, "What does it mean to say a church is safe?" Sadly, many will answer, "A safe church is one where people don't know what I'm really like." In fact, I fear that if you knew me as I really am, you would run from me. If you knew the struggles, the evil thoughts, the selfish motives, and the unloving actions that I wrestle with on a daily basis, you would be so repulsed you would walk away.

Because of fear, we've erected a facade of secrecy and called it safety. Churches have aided and abetted this illusion by producing environments where no one really wants to know what's going on in your soul. We're content when people show up, give, and serve. If you have personal problems, don't tell us—see a therapist. The result? Untouched lives—no community.

The safety I long for allows me to be real, to share my struggles, my fears, my failures—*and* to believe you'll accept me. Yes, the desire for safety is the longing that cries out, "Accept me."

TO KNOW YOU'RE FOR ME

Several years ago I shared with a friend how finances have been an ongoing source of struggle during my adult life. Managing money, budgeting, and keeping good records aren't my strong points. This has been a source of personal embarrassment as well as the cause of many heated arguments at home.

After I shared this with my friend, I feared he would reject me. The information I shared lay dormant for a long time in our relationship. I heard an occasional, "How are things going?"—seldom more than that. Then my worst nightmare came true. He'd heard a few rumors that stoked a smoldering fire of suspicion, until it blazed into a strong expression of concern for my family, my ministry, and me. Then he dropped the bomb: "So I'm getting out. I'm leaving before the ship goes down." After it exploded, he walked out, and I sat stunned. I wanted to run, but I couldn't. It was several minutes before I realized tears were flowing down my cheeks.

A part of me said, "I'll never let this happen again." If I'm not real with you, if I don't expose my life, you can't hurt me, and I won't be rejected. And yet to live that way would deny the very environment God created me to live in and enjoy. The tension was like a heavy barbell sitting on my chest.

Four days later, a friend flew into town, and we were planning to take a drive together up into the mountains. I had been agonizing over whether I would share with him what had happened. No one would fault me for being gun-shy. Who could blame me for keeping it to myself? So why did I feel a pull to share not only the disappointing reaction I'd been handed but also the financial struggles still present in my life?

Could the words of Hebrews 10—about encouraging and stirring up one another to love better and live better—really be lived out? As I picked my friend up at the airport, I resolved to find out.

After mutually catching up, I launched into a monologue of what I had feared sharing. The miles rolled by, and my words moved beyond Monday's story as I opened up about the struggles and failures that are part of my journey. I wanted to keep talking. I was terrified to hear his reaction. When I finally ran out of words, there was silence. I remember stealing a glance and seeing my friend staring out the window. As he continued to look at the passing countryside, he quietly said, "Nothing you've said or could say would cause me to give up on you and walk away."

I tear up as I remember that. I experienced safety that day, and it penetrated deeply.

SO WILL I

My soul longs for true safety—not tolerance, not overlooking sin, but the safety of experiencing this acceptance the gospel makes possible. The safety of that community with my friend reached deeper than the earlier sting of abandonment.

In a safe community, the passion to celebrate grace is released. Philip Yancey, in *What's So Amazing About Grace,* calls grace "the last best word." He adds: "Grace means there is nothing we can do to make God love us more…. And grace means there is nothing we can do to make God love us less."[1]

When a church, a small group, or even two friends embrace safety, something good is released; grace is celebrated. I begin to live out the new purity that the new covenant gives me. All my filth, all the ugliness of my sin is no longer held against me because a loving God has washed me clean by the blood of His Son. He accepts me as I am and where I am, and what I do or don't do won't change that acceptance. It's based on His Son, not my performance.

What do we do when a friend has failed? How do we react to news of moral failure? Is there shock? "I can't believe John would do that." Is there judgment? "I can tell you this: He won't be accepted here anymore." Is there sadness? "I can hardly bear thinking about what these choices will mean in his life."

There's a place for shock, a place for standards, a place for sadness. But a place of safety offers more: It invites my friend to abandon his facade in honestly confessing his failures or struggles, believing and hoping that because his heavenly Father accepts him, so will I.

We Will Celebrate

We're experiencing this safety as a church community. Despite the pain and because of the joy in my own experiences, in our church's worship times I extend the call for safety in two ways. One is through my preaching. I present my life as a fellow struggler on the journey. My vulnerability is a means to point people to Christ, to model the celebration of grace. I don't share everything. I share enough to let people know I depend on grace—and they can too. That gives people permission to share the struggles of their own lives.

Second, on a regular basis, we incorporate a season of prayer into our worship time. We invite people to leave their seats and come to the front to pray with one of our leaders. I've often heard confessions of struggles that are raw and fresh.

One such time involved a husband struggling with marital faithfulness. Our prayer that morning led to a conversation later in the week in my office. I asked him what prompted his coming down to pray with me and tell me his struggles. He answered, "I'd heard you mention in a recent sermon that you and your wife struggled at times in your marriage, so it felt safe to ask for your prayers and your help."

In recent days, my soul has drawn refreshment from a place I probably had never before explored. The words come from Zephaniah; they are words that celebrate grace.

The LORD your God is with you, he is mighty to save. He
will take great delight in you, he will quiet you with his
love, he will rejoice over you with singing.[2]

It's the picture of a God who accepts me, delights in me, and sings over
me. I don't ever want to lose sight of this truth and the hope it brings.
Amazing! He knows me better than anyone, and He still delights and sings.

Is it possible for this to be a picture of the church? When we're released
to be community to one another, when we allow the atmosphere of safety
to permeate our preaching, our small groups, and our relationships, then
we'll stir one another with the passion of grace. We will celebrate Christ,
moving in and through our fellow strugglers.

As I write, I'm reminded of those rich moments riding with a friend
who delighted and sang over me. You might understand how such a thing
could happen with one friend, but you wonder: "Could it ever happen in
a church?"

In the past year, I took that risk all over again, only this time with the
ten men of my small group, ten men who have come to see me as I really
am—a man who struggles, a man who needs a safe place to be accepted.
What happened in that group makes me eager to explore with you the next
word that defines community. First *safety*...now *vision*.

5

Vision

Be Thou my vision, O Lord of my heart,
Naught be all else to me save that Thou art;
Thou my best thought by day or by night,
Waking or sleeping, Thy presence my light.

IRISH HYMN, EIGHTH CENTURY

It is so easy to think that the Church has a lot of different objects—education, building, missions, holding services.... The Church exists for no other purpose but to draw men into Christ, to make them little Christs. If they are not doing that, all the cathedrals, clergy, missions, sermons, even the Bible itself, are simply a waste of time. God became man for no other purpose. It is even doubtful, you know, whether the whole universe was created for any other reason.

C. S. LEWIS

W here there is no vision, the people perish."[1] And, "for such a time as this."[2] These two verses have perhaps jump-started more church building campaigns and new programs than we can imagine. Ripped out of Scripture with little regard for context, they've become the catalyst for the American church to define vision.

Several years ago, I was called to perform a wedding in another part of the country. As I arrived at the church for the rehearsal, I was met by the wedding director. Though friendly enough, she left me with little doubt as to who was in charge. We engaged in typical conversation while waiting for the rehearsal to begin. I asked about the church and how long she'd been there. The more she talked, the more her sense of excitement became evident. As our conversation ended, she asked if I would be staying for Sunday's service.

My no brought a disappointed look to her face and an unspoken "too bad" to her lips. So I asked: "What's so special about Sunday?" (If a big giveaway were scheduled, maybe I'd change my plans and stay.)

That was all the encouragement she needed. With great animation she announced that Pastor Smith, this Sunday, was going to share the vision God had given him concerning their new building campaign. The church already had plans to expand the campus, including a worship area that would seat thousands. But now "God had shown the pastor" that the original blueprint wasn't large enough.

"God has shown the pastor"—curious, isn't it, that God's visions invariably mean "bigger and better."

WHO YOU CAN BE

We recently built a worship center on our campus. For fourteen years we'd been using our gym. Then came the critical congregational meeting we needed for approval. Well into the meeting, a member asked whether I thought the building was a direction from the Lord. My response: "It makes sense." I went on to say that we'd spent considerable time praying, drawing plans, and exhausting all the details involved in the project. Compare "It makes sense" to "God spoke to me." What I said somehow didn't feel as compelling.

For me, spiritual vision centers on the gospel truth that God is at work in a believer's life. Vision is the realization of who you *can* be. That realization leads to the refusal to give up on people, to never discard them.

We're terrified to be known, to be exposed. If you knew *this* about me, would you see me as hopeless? Would you give up on me?

Vision is the ability to turn weapons of exposure into tools of encouragement. The qualities of safety, vision, wisdom, and power are best seen in progression, building on one another.

SAFETY → VISION

As safety answers the heart cry of "Accept me," so vision answers the cry, "Don't discard me; instead view me with a commitment to realize who I can become—believe in me."

The believer in a new covenant church hears, "It's safe to be real because I have a vision for your life." Paul had this vision for the communities to whom he ministered. Hear his passion:

> My dear children, for whom I am again in the pains of childbirth until Christ is formed in you.[3]

> …that we may present everyone perfect in Christ. To this end I labor, struggling with all his energy, which so powerfully works in me.[4]

Paul's energy, passion, and effort were poured into people's lives with a vision for who they could be as they understood the new way to live and relate, made possible by the new covenant:

> My purpose is that they may be encouraged in heart and
> united in love, so that they may have the full riches of com-
> plete understanding, in order that they may know the mys-
> tery of God, namely, Christ, in whom are hidden all the
> treasures of wisdom and knowledge.[5]

This is the grid through which I view people. The reality of Christ and the treasures placed in us through Him are the bases for shaping the vision of who someone can be. It affects how I see my wife and daughters, the board members with whom I serve, and the congregation I pastor. As I observe their lives, my thoughts focus in this direction:

"They have a relationship with Christ. Because of that, I know they live with a new purity, they have a new identity (they're children of God). They possess a new heart inclined toward Christ, and they're energized with the power of the Holy Spirit. Therefore, what do I envision as their potential? I long to see them—and me—more fully released to be who we already are."

WAITING FOR CHRIST TO BE FORMED

One board member challenges every new direction our church takes. He offers critical comments to any who will listen. So I'm faced with a choice. Do I scheme to outmaneuver his challenges? Do I turn them into power struggles? Do I become passive and simply hang on until his term is up?

Or do I have the passion and insight to envision who he could be if the marks of a new covenant believer were released in his irritating life?

My wife and I have faced a similar challenge in the lives of our daughters. They're young women now (twenty-five, twenty-four, and twenty-one), but as they were growing up, they did their share of questioning life and pushing boundaries. We've faced the challenge of keeping their potential in view while at the same time guiding, correcting, and disciplining. It's never easy.

Several years ago I opened a phone bill and stared in disbelief. The payment due was over $300. My eyes quickly scanned the breakdown and came to rest on one line—a phone call of 260 minutes! I'm no math whiz, but that's more than four hours. Did I begin to envision who my daughter could be and spend time quietly reflecting on the marks of the new covenant in her life? NO! I quickly and not so quietly found her, presented her the bill to pay, and asked, "What in the world could you possibly talk about for four hours?"

During that same time, Suzi and I were out of town for a weekend and had left two of our daughters at home. We were crossing the bridge that many parents do of trusting them to live in our absence according to our clear rules and expectations. The phone rang and the call began, "Dad, I know you're going to be mad, but let me explain…" Clear rules had been violated. People had been in our home who shouldn't have been there, and the police had been called. Not exactly the phone call we wanted.

In the hours that followed, on our instantly scheduled return trip home, many thoughts crossed our minds. What would our response be? Homicide was ruled out fairly quickly. Then we ran through other options. While we were away, I had been teaching on the four marks of a new covenant church. Both our daughters were, and are, believers. What would our response look like if we viewed their behavior with the reality of the new covenant in mind? When we sat with them, the conversation reflected the thrilling truth that we had a vision for them. There were consequences, of course, but we conveyed our stubborn vision for who they could become as the reality of Christ was realized in their lives. We felt a burden akin to pregnancy as we waited for Christ to be formed in them.

THEY SAW WHO I COULD BE

In a safe community, people can be real because a vision exists for them. That *theological* reality became a *personal* reality for me in my Wednesday morning small group.

I mentioned earlier my ongoing struggle with finances. The struggle ebbs and flows, but it's always there. Several months ago, the waves pounded my life. In fact, a tidal wave poured in. I pictured myself, shovel in hand, furiously digging. Suddenly, I saw myself in the bottom of a deep hole with no way out. For twenty-four hours I wrestled with this image that reflected my battle with money. I couldn't shake the thought, *Share this burden with the men of the Wednesday morning group.* I can still recall the fear: Would they reject me? Would they sit in judgment? Perhaps they would say, "With struggles like that, you have no business being a pastor."

I decided to send an e-mail to two of the guys along with a weak "Pray for me; I'm struggling." I pushed the send button and held my breath. Soon a message popped up: UNDELIVERABLE—SYSTEMS ERROR. Relief! A sign from God!

My next choice: Call and hope to get their voicemail. I did, and left the simple undefined request I'd attempted to send via e-mail. Later that day, the return calls came. Both men were willing to pray, but they wanted to meet me for coffee to hear more. My heart began to race. I mumbled, "Okay."

As we had coffee, the floodgates of my heart burst open. I began to trace the struggle. Strangely, the anxiety disappeared as I looked into their eyes. When they finally replied, their words stirred me to think of what could be, who I could be. I'd made mistakes, consequences existed, that was clear. But there was so much more. *They actually believed in me.* More important, they saw who I could be if Christ were released in my financial life. Ugliness and all, it hadn't caused rejection or judgment. Once again I left aroused to love better and to live better.

Taste the Possibilities

These men, along with the others who heard my story, worked together to write me a vision letter. Imagine how I felt when I read these words:

> We see a man at *peace.* The peace that we see is a peace that
> doesn't come easily to you. It's a peace that comes from
> knowing God will provide for ALL your needs. He loves
> you enough that He'll never let you come to a place of
> comfort providing for your needs and wants yourself—and
> with His help, and ours, you'll struggle (well) with this.
>
> We see a man who's *content.* God *has* met your needs,
> God *does* meet your needs, and God *will* meet all your needs.
> His grace is sufficient for you. The things of this world will
> NEVER bring contentment to you. Any contentment you

feel you have in these things is merely counterfeit. Only His grace and love can meet your needs. We see in you a man who can rest in this.

We see a man who's *free*. Free from the burden of resentment from injustices of the past. Free from a constant sense of indebtedness to anyone else but God. Free from sleepless nights wondering how ends will meet. Free from Essex Fells and the need to compete. Free to forgive and be forgiven. Free to drive in the slow lane. Free to study and pray without interruption from the demons of the past. Free to write. Free to preach. Free to love.

We see a man who knows *joy*. Beyond and through the struggle with life is the joy that puts the struggle into focus. We see in you a man who sees through the struggles—not just because you know this is true, but more importantly, because you've experienced it to be true. We see a man whose joy frees him from the overwhelming burden of making ends meet. As a result of this, you can be free to laugh with your family, knowing full well that God's love for you, shown through your love for them, is sufficient.

Churches can be released to become communities. They can be vital in the lives of strugglers. My prayer is that your soul can begin to taste the possibilities. *Safety* to be real. *Vision* to become.

Next...we need *wisdom*.

6

Wisdom

There is a mine for silver

and a place where gold is refined....

Man puts an end to the darkness;

he searches the farthest recesses

for ore in the blackest darkness....

He searches the sources of the rivers

and brings hidden things to light.

But where can wisdom be found?

JOB 28:1,3,11-12

Know anyone who qualifies as wise? For me, the list is short. I know many smart people, and I know a lot who are successful, but the names of people I would call wise don't easily come to mind. From the ancient times of Job to current culture, wisdom remains in short supply.

I wonder if we offset the shortage of wisdom by redefining it to make it more accessible, more easily manufactured. In our world of instant everything, waiting for something of value is unacceptable. Some therefore look at success and call it wisdom.

CRAVING SUCCESS

Our appetite for success is insatiable. The person who starts with little and builds an empire is prized and praised. Our love affair with success permeates all aspects of our culture. Even in the church subculture, wisdom and success are often confused.

Scan ads in Christian periodicals and you'll reach this conclusion: Success can be yours. If you need to know how to market your church, try this or that program. Christian leaders need to sort their way through the complexities of running a church, so earn a degree in organizational skills.

At a recent pastors' conference, I was asked if I'd hired a coach yet. My puzzled expression prompted the questioner to explain that this was "the latest management strategy." One church even went to corporate America to find the "right" coach.

Listen to how we describe churches. Our words ooze success: "Fastest growing church in the Southwest." "Largest in their denomination." "The church with the key to reaching the next generation." Our local paper recently reviewed a book that identifies the top one hundred churches in America. By what criteria? Success at something visible.

We crave success! When you achieve success, you write a book, host a conference, and tell others "how to do it." They'll come sit at your feet, they'll learn, they'll imitate, and all the while they'll think they're acquiring wisdom.

To See and to Challenge

There's a better way to wisdom—a better way whether yours is a church of one hundred, one thousand, or ten thousand; a better way whether you're Baptist or Episcopalian or charismatic. In this better way, supernatural living is nurtured, the resources of the new covenant are released, and a community of people walk the spiritual journey together. The marks of this community flow with supernatural rhythm. And the challenges we truly long for and were made for will be placed before us.

Safety declares, "We accept you." Vision pledges, "We believe in what you can become." Then comes wisdom, which promises, "We'll challenge you." If we're to reach the vision of becoming like Jesus in a safe community of grace, wisdom must be operative.

SAFETY $\rightarrow$ VISION $\rightarrow$ WISDOM

For our hearts cry out not only "Accept me" and "Believe in me" but also "Challenge me."

Wisdom is essential for change. Paul told the Ephesian believers that he was praying for them,

> asking God, the glorious Father of our Lord Jesus Christ,
> to give you spiritual wisdom and understanding, so that
> you might grow in your knowledge of God.[1]

True wisdom, spiritual wisdom, leads to change by challenging us in two ways. First, wisdom involves discernment. Before we challenge, we see into someone's soul and discern the obstacles that keep that person from growing in the image of Christ. Wisdom sees both the problem and the potential. Second, wisdom encourages the qualities of Christ that are already present in someone's life, then nurtures them toward richer expression.

When safety is valued and vision is growing, wisdom is then free to challenge, and transformation takes place. This transformation includes the ability to view life with God's perspective, to seek to make sense of life with its difficulties, injustices, and struggles—and to still trust in God when we fail to understand. It means seeking after Him and all He has promised.

Wisdom longs for the resources of the new covenant to transform the inner being. And it longs for God to be known—a knowing that includes both the objective truth of who He is and the subjective reality of experiencing Him in everyday life.

FIRST, DISCERNMENT

If we eliminate discernment—if we don't worry about seeing deeply into the inner being—our efforts at transformation become moralism. Wisdom is no longer necessary; simply learn the rules and conform. When that happens in a church, the atmosphere turns deadly. Our focus spotlights external standards, and our dominant experience in community becomes pressure and judgment. Acceptance is granted only when standards are met.

Many prefer rules and their application over wisdom. Often we're afraid to let wisdom challenge our deep sinfulness in the context of safety and vision. In the church context we're fearful that sin will get out of control, that people will get away with all kinds of wrongdoing with no one to stop them. Too often, churches want pastors who will act as moral policemen in the lives of their people. Find the offense, confront it, then remove the offense or the person.

Too often that's the church's standard operating procedure. The result is profound guilt, mounting pressure, and thickening walls of secrecy.

Listen to the lethal realities that echo in a recent letter I received:

Dear Pastor Kallam,

I've been a Christian since my teens. I haven't struggled so much with my belief but with how my belief was played out in everyday life. I've tried various plans, strategies, and programs that are offered in books and magazines. I've tried forcing myself into a routine or discipline that didn't fit. Then, when these various plans failed, I would feel even worse due to my lack of discipline.

More recently through what I've heard you teach and what I'm learning about what God has done for me, that is changing. I don't want anymore of the to-do list kind of Christianity. I want a relationship based on an under-standing of who He is and who I am in Him.

There really is a better way! Talk in this way, however, and you can count on one thing—you'll be misunderstood. I've lost count of the times I've been told, "Kallam, you're soft on sin."

Here's one example, a recent one. As I answered the phone, it quickly became evident the call would not be pleasant. My emotions ranged from disbelief to anger to sadness. The woman on the other end, a member of our church, was upset. She was convinced—and others shared her view, she added—that I had little if any concern for my daughters' spiritual lives. Her overwhelming "proof" of my failure included a movie I'd mentioned we saw (one she regarded as unacceptable), the fact that my daughters didn't attend a particular program at church, and my wife's noninvolvement in a particular Bible study group.

MY CHOICE

Note it well: When wisdom isn't applied to deal with the struggles of life or with our sin, we become moralists, and legalism becomes the atmosphere of our community.

Ten years ago, I made a choice to pursue wisdom that flows out of grace instead of managing people into guilt-inspired conformity. That choice shapes the way I relate to people. It recognizes that transformation is first an inner-world process. Real transformation, where we become more like Christ as wisdom removes obstacles and nurtures new life in our hearts, is a lifelong process. Real transformation depends on what Christ has secured for me and on my new desires that struggle against my old ones. When wisdom is at work, who I am and how I live aligns with the life of Jesus.

This kind of wisdom rests on three realities that shape our relational interactions:

- *Value:* who each of us is because of what Christ has done.
- *Confidence:* in who I am and in what I have to offer others because of what Christ has done.
- *Strength:* to move into others' lives with courage and passion because of what Christ has done.

56

INNER-WORLD TRANSFORMATION

Several years ago, Alex came to me to confess his plight and get help. He struggled with Internet pornography. It had become a growing part of his world, though he loved both his wife and kids and was also in a leadership role in our ministry.

Since that time, I've seen that same scenario and similar ones played out many times in other lives. It happens in *your* church community as well. What do you do?

I remember sitting with Alex. As he was talking, I quietly asked God for wisdom. Of course his choices were sinful. No question there. Was my role simply to say, "Stop it"? We could take steps to limit his Internet access and set up an accountability partner. But listen carefully: If that were all I did, then wisdom wouldn't be operative and inner-world transformation would never take place.

When Alex finished sharing with me his plight, he looked at me, waiting for my response. I felt pressure to fix the problem, but I went deeper into my own soul in search of spiritual wisdom. He didn't need me to deliver a sermon on the evils of pornography; he needed something to overcome that evil.

"Do you wonder what God thinks of you?" I asked.

His eyes got big. "What?" he blurted.

I repeated my question.

"How should I know?" he responded. "You're the pastor!" Then, after a pause, he quietly added, "I guess He doesn't think much of me."

As Alex listened, I began to paint a picture of not only his value to God but also the realities Christ had placed in him as a result of the new covenant. I talked of how those realities are deeper in his soul than any desire to look at pornography. I ended by offering to walk on his journey with him. Together we would seek to understand the pull of the pornography, but more than that, we would explore a vision of inner-world transformation that would draw him away from broken cisterns and lead him to living water.

We've been walking through that process now for several years. The pornography at times still presents a temptation, but there's a growing likeness to Christ in Alex. Alex is discovering wisdom in an atmosphere of safety and vision.

Safety. Vision. Wisdom. Three marks of spiritual community. There's one more. Without it, no lasting change will occur: *Power.*

7

Power

We must never allow anything to interfere with the consecration of
our spiritual power. Consecration (being dedicated to God's ser-
vice) is our part; sanctification (being set apart from sin and being
made holy) is God's part. We must make a deliberate determina-
tion to be interested only in what God is interested.

Oswald Chambers

Every year Charlotte hosts two NASCAR races. Hundreds of thousands of people attend, and millions of dollars pour into our local
economy. In connection with the races, the local paper does an annual feature titled "The Twenty-Five Most Powerful Faces of NASCAR." These
people are called powerful because they shape the present and the future of
this vast empire of stock-car racing.

What makes someone powerful? Powerful people are sprinkled through
every arena in life. From NASCAR to Hollywood, from government to big
business, movers and shakers are everywhere. In each case, criteria are used

to define what makes them so powerful. The church is no exception. It isn't immune to this world of power.

In the church, we often think that power resides in strong personalities or strong programs. A person with power acquires a growing sphere of influence that cycles back, reinforcing the power. The cycle is a vicious one, with ever-increasing expectations to perform and perform well. More than once a well-meaning member of our church has commented after a sermon, "Wow, Jim, you really hit a home run with that message!" As I'd process that compliment, my mind would race. Does he mean most of my sermons are only singles or, even worse, weak pop-ups? Is he saying that, whatever I did, I'd *better* do it again? The pressure mounts as weeks turn into months and the member never again tells me I hit a home run.

A couple I counsel calls to tell me nothing is working. They won't be coming in anymore—they're getting a divorce. As I hang up, I don't feel very powerful. I feel weak and ineffective.

POWER CRITERIA

What criteria define power? What standards am I using to evaluate my own life and ministry?

If the criteria for defining power are found in certain personality types, polished sermons, the newest program, or the percentage of counseling success—most pastors are in trouble. We don't measure up. The pressure escalates, and either we go into scramble mode to stay one step ahead, or we resign ourselves to the fact that we won't make the grade.

New covenant communities see power differently. To them, power completes a path: one that, when all four marks are evident, releases the church to become a new covenant community where true Holy Spirit enablement is poured out of Spirit-filled people.

That final mark of a new covenant community, power, is only released when we recognize our own weakness and surrender to the Holy Spirit.

SAFETY → VISION → WISDOM → POWER

Our hearts cry out, "Accept me, believe in me, challenge me...and *pour into me.*"

Dwight Edwards writes, "This new power from God's Spirit is the same power that raised Christ from the dead. It is also the new power that *alone* can resurrect us from the defeated, death-like quality of life to which our flesh seeks to hold us in bondage."[1]

It's a fact that we struggle with our flesh. As we recognize the reality that this struggle is a supernatural one, we admit that to struggle well requires a power source beyond our natural strength. And that new covenant power source is the Holy Spirit. "I will put my Spirit in you."[2] so that you can "serve in the new way of the Spirit"[3]—because it is the "Spirit [who] gives life."[4] God has poured His Spirit *into* my life, and as His life-giving Spirit permeates my being, His power pours *out* of my new life and *into* my new covenant community. Now that's a cycle I want to see in my church!

Jesus describes this with a vivid word picture: "Whoever believes in me, as the Scripture has said, streams of living water will flow from within him." And the gospel writer adds, "By this he meant the Spirit."[5] Think of it. I have this life-giving power living in me. So do you, if you know Jesus. We could become a powerful community.

WHY DOESN'T IT CHANGE?

I sat in the office of a friend as he poured out his heart's struggle. "Why is it that even though I've been a Christian for more than thirty years, I still struggle with the same sin issues?" In confusion and desperation he went on, "Why isn't the Holy Spirit working? I pray and ask God; I just don't seem to be able to get it right."

It was a familiar situation someone else has described well:

> No matter what their struggle is, all of these people have this in common: They're bound, snared into slavery by a besetting sin. They feel chained, unable to break free from sin's power.
>
> Many of these dear people sincerely love Jesus. They have prayed diligently, cried a river of tears, sought counseling from pastors and friends. Yet nothing seems to free them. They always end up going back to their sin. And their heavy burden of guilt only increases with time.[6]

Confusion and frustration fill so many of our private worlds. That day it was my friend who was struggling and asking the questions, but it could just as easily have been me. I frequently face similar confusion. Henri Nouwen's words give expression to the confusion that rages in my soul:

> In solitude I get rid of my scaffolding: no friends to talk with, no telephone calls to make, no meetings to attend, no music to entertain, no books to distract, just me—naked,

vulnerable, weak, sinful, deprived, broken—nothing.… As
soon as I decide to stay in my solitude, confusing ideas,
disturbing images, wild fantasies, and weird associations
jump about in my mind like monkeys in a banana tree.[7]

In response to Nouwen's words, I wrote the following: *Why won't it change? The wild ugly thoughts Nouwen describes are present in my times of solitude too. Perhaps I don't linger long enough to break through, to have the thoughts vanish. Relief seems an illusion. God appears ineffective to provide peace and contentment. I feel powerless to live differently. I want the power to be released in me that will allow me to live free from guilt, criticism, and judgment.*

You may be thinking, *And he's a pastor?* But you'll see in the following story how in my weakness the Holy Spirit was released in community. Many years ago a young man began attending our church as a new believer, full of questions. Recently, he shared two radically different experiences that have marked his journey. Years earlier he attended a men's breakfast where I was speaking. He reflected, "I naively asked you what the Holy Spirit had done in your life that week." Bill said my look was one of shock, and the response of the men around him was to rebuff him for asking. He felt different and excluded.

In contrast, he described a more recent time when he heard me say that I don't understand the mysteries of how the Spirit works, yet I long to know the Spirit better. Bill summed it up this way: "It's this kind of vulnerability that breeds inclusion, mostly because it reflects a truth of spiritual transformation. We all struggle in growing to know Him. This has been the beginning of community for me and has transformed my life."

BANKRUPT

What does it take to release the Spirit in my life? When I understand how that works, what will it look like in the life of my community?

Fundamental to answering those questions is the understanding that God has already poured His life-giving Spirit into me. The power is already present. We aren't waiting for another experience to make us powerful. Paul admonished the Galatian believers not to live foolishly, and he asked, "Are you now trying to attain your goal [living for God] by human effort?"[8] In effect Paul was saying, live the way you began. The Spirit was given not to honor my effort but to keep God's promise.

As I ponder this, a picture begins to develop in my mind. It's a picture of bankruptcy. I'm standing before a judge, my pockets turned inside out and empty. I have nothing to offer. Jesus framed the situation in the first of the Beatitudes: "Blessed are the poor in spirit."[9] What a picture! People are favored by God when they acknowledge spiritual bankruptcy. They find a wealth of happiness in abject poverty. I embrace utter dependence on God when I realize I bring nothing.

Living in the Spirit's power is about releasing what God has already provided; it's not about manufacturing a way of life by strenuous effort. Whether I rest or strain depends on how I believe change will take place. In *Beside a Quiet Stream,* Penelope Stokes explains it this way:

> The change doesn't come because we work at it, because we
> grit our teeth and clench our fists and will it into existence.
> It doesn't happen because we pray for it day and night,
> study how to get it, or make it happen by the force of our
> conviction.

It's a gift from the heart of the Creator, a grace
bestowed by the One who loves us.[10]

It would be so much simpler if we could just produce an ironclad, easy-to-follow method to produce spiritual power. Many claim that such methods exist, yet when held up to human experience as well as to Scripture, they are found wanting. And that's good news. It's part of the gospel. The pressure is off to "make it happen." God's promise of the indwelling Spirit has been ful-filled in the bankrupt lives of all who are recipients of the new covenant.

In *The River Within,* Jeff Imbach writes of "a deeper, integrated spiritu-ality" that we can discover "if we hold on to the call to love God with all our hearts and insist on learning how to live passionately in the world."[11] The answer lies in acknowledging my bankruptcy before God, embracing the passionate capacity to love God, and allowing the Spirit to be released in my life.

Giving Up

After our daughter Jackie graduated from high school, she began to test the boundaries of life with us. She began college while living at home. Her lifestyle choices soon put her at odds with us, and the relationship between us began to disintegrate. The patterns of her life became destructive, at least to us. Suzi and I were scared and didn't know what to do.

In the days we faced those struggles, the word that best described my interior world was *scrambled.* Our world was spinning out of control, and nothing I was doing made a difference. I stayed awake late at night schem-ing—thinking of new strategies to bring Jackie back to her senses and out of danger.

Months into the struggle I remember praying, *Lord, I've had it. I give up. I'm tired of trying to make this work—I put Jackie into your hands.*

Jackie worked through her battles and recently spent six months at a Bible school in New Zealand. (Go figure!) I received a Father's Day card from her while she was there. In it she expressed thanks for what she felt for me during her time of wandering:

> Dad, thanks for being the father you are. I know the only
> reason that you are who you are is because of Christ living
> in you. I don't understand how God can love me and that
> He can forgive me—but He does. Sometimes I don't know
> how you could love me and forgive me—but I know you
> do. Thank you for being an example of Christ's love.
>
> Love, Jackie

As I wiped away the tears, I knew that whatever love Jackie felt was born out of the power of the Holy Spirit being released in me. During those dark days my spirit wanted to punish and hurt anyone who got in my way. It was only as the Spirit of the living God was released that life-giving community was poured into our daughter's life.

As I live in this reality, I'm freed to pour into the lives of others with power. In a powerful new covenant community, people pour what is most supernaturally alive in their own souls into the souls of others. The result is movement toward spiritual formation.

PART THREE

Intentional Community

Friendship

A friend loves at all times.

PROVERBS 17:17

There is a friend who sticks closer than a brother.

PROVERBS 18:24

Above all, love each other deeply, because love covers over a multitude of sins.

1 PETER 4:8

R ecently Suzi and I sat with another couple in a fine restaurant and enjoyed a wonderful evening. The setting was simple yet elegant. Our table occupied a delightful spot near a large window overlooking a lake. Tablecloths, candlelight, and soft jazz completed the picture. The food presentation was pleasing, and the taste, delicious. However, none of that was what made the evening memorable.

The couple with us had been our friends for twenty-seven years. In fact, the reason for that dinner was to celebrate our friendship. Our whole adult journey has included the four of us walking together. We've shared the joys of children's births, of first homes purchased, vacations, graduations, dance recitals, and countless meals. We've shed tears over loved ones dying, a job change that took them out of Charlotte for eight years, and disappointments of many kinds. We've shared our lives, good and bad.

At times we wondered if the friendship would survive. The struggles have been real, sometimes severe. And yet not only has our relationship survived, it has flourished.

Around that table by the lake, we remembered and celebrated and also envisioned what might yet come. As the evening ended, Suzi and I gave four gifts to our friends. The first two were vision letters, one from Suzi to the wife, another from me to the husband. The letters were born out of years of walking together, seeing God at work in their lives, and envisioning what God longs for them to be and to know.

The final gifts represented the vision in the letters. Suzi gave her friend a crystal bowl to symbolize her vision of pure beauty, sparkling because it had been washed clean. I gave the husband a geode, symbolizing outer strength wrapped around an inner beauty that comes from Christ.

Lasting Friendship

Community like that which I've described in this book is accomplished in large measure through the building of spiritual friendships with people who will involve themselves with one another in the long process of spiritual formation. In spiritual formation, the inner life of Jesus, over time, becomes visible in my life. It's who I am, what I do, and how I live my life.

I need friends—and so do you—who hear the call from God expressed in Hebrews: "Consider how we may spur one another on toward love and good deeds.... Let us encourage one another."[1] These friends are eager to experience Christ's life released in others. So they intentionally—moving with purpose—seek to incite and arouse a passion for Christ within us. They invest in our lives to release us to live willingly for the glory of God.

There are many qualities that characterize a friend. In the margins of this page, you could list a number of friendship qualities that are important to you. My own boiled-down list includes these top two qualities: My heart longs for friendships that are *lasting* and friendships where *love expressed* is the prominent feature.

All of us have experienced friendships lost. The pain we feel is enormous when someone we thought would be a friend for a long time just walks away. They take the path of least resistance when situations become difficult. Perhaps you've not only experienced this happening to you, but have also done it to someone else.

The cry of Job has been the cry of my heart more than once:

> A despairing man should have the devotion of his friends,
>   even though he forsakes the fear of the Almighty.
> But my brothers are as undependable as intermittent
>   streams.[2]

Friendship requires the ability to see a friend at his or her worst and look beyond all that is ugly to what could be. It's standing with someone in the darkest of nights and allowing the light of Christ to pierce that darkness.

There are times, I know, when it's hard, really hard, to be my friend. I'm sometimes self-absorbed and demanding. In my pettiness, I push people away. The silence is often deafening. A spiritual friend will hang in and not give up. I long for that friend. I have several. I long to be that friend. Sometimes I am.

LOVE EXPRESSED

My second favorite quality for friendship is love expressed.

I have a living picture of this in our youngest daughter, Graylyn. I have observed her, time and time again, hanging in there with her friends. In situations and relationships where I would have been tempted to walk away, she persevered. One such time she told a friend, "You've hurt me, and even though I'm scared, I want our friendship to go forward." When I asked her why she responded like that, she said, "Dad, she's my friend. I love her."

Perhaps that attitude centers on the ability to overlook an offense.

> He who covers over an offense promotes love,
> > but whoever repeats the matter separates close friends.[3]

> Above all, love each other deeply, because love covers over a
> multitude of sins.[4]

In the passages above, both Solomon and Peter strongly state that there's a place for covering over an offense. Love tolerates mistakes and forgives wrongs. Love actively demonstrated is prominent ("above all") and must be intentionally pursued ("love each other deeply").

The therapeutic world we live in sometimes suggests the opposite.

We're told that for healing to take place, wrongs done to you by another need to be found, exposed, and aggressively addressed with that person. If you've hurt me, you *will* know about it. Likewise, our churches, even our small groups, are many times places where license has been given to open fire in the name of honesty and truth.

Scripture aims us in a different direction. I can choose to forget how a friend has wronged me, because of love.

There's no formula for knowing when to confront and when to cover over an offense. Spirit-driven wisdom, born out of a safe environment, becomes the only true guide for such a decision. I must trust the Spirit in my heart, and I can trust Him if my heart knows the depths of forgiveness already extended to me.

I have a friend who, many times, switches his brain off before speaking. Words flow without any awareness of their barbed content or, more significantly, of their impact on people. On many occasions I've been left thinking, *Does he know what he just said? Does he realize how hurtful that is?*

Recently, at a party, he spouted off about people in ministry, in particular about pastors. When he finished, throats were uncomfortably cleared, and an awkward silence descended. I felt eyes turning toward me as if to ask, "How are you going to respond?"

At that moment I had a choice. I felt hurt and embarrassed by what he said. Anger was present, but so were other feelings. This was a friend I cared for and who I knew cared for me. I let the comments go, choosing instead to promote love.

Maybe you're shaking your head as you read this. Perhaps you think I let him get away with a wrong that should have been righted. In my mind, grace was extended. What flooded through me at that moment was the brokenness of my own heart and how much I need and long for grace. And

I remembered as well that I'm nothing if I don't love. As a line from Eugene Peterson's paraphrase of 1 Corinthians 13 puts it, "No matter what I say, what I believe, and what I do, I'm bankrupt without love."[5]

FOUR STEPPING STONES

Lasting friendships where love is prominently demonstrated follow a path. Four stones make up this path. (I first heard this idea from Larry Crabb.) As we seek to release the church to become a community, these four stones provide good solid footing:

CURIOSITY → BROKENNESS → BOLDNESS → DEPENDENCE

The path begins with intrigue, with a willingness to be *curious* about a friend's life. Do I desire to know you? Will I leave my world of self-absorption and wonder what God is doing in your life? As long as I'm wrapped up in my life, my needs, my struggles, and my dreams, I won't be curious about yours.

Several years ago a friend came to our home for dinner. His ministry was growing and highly visible (you would probably recognize his name), and we looked forward to this opportunity for catching up on each other's lives. From the moment we greeted him until he left, *we* asked questions and *he* told stories. Then he left.

As Suzi and I were getting ready for bed, she was muttering to herself, opening and closing drawers with great emphasis, and generally appearing agitated. Perceptive husband that I am, I asked, "Is something wrong?"

"You bet there is," came the reply. Suzi went on to state what had been obvious to her. Our friend had never asked one question about our lives.

There had been no curiosity about our ministry, no interest in our daughters or anything about us. Both of us felt dishonored, a feeling that could have degenerated into whining. But the feeling was legitimate—we all long to be known.

Friendship begins with a curiosity to know another. Our questions will relate not only to external happenings but will also probe internal awareness. A friend wonders what God is up to in another's life.

The next stone I step on is *brokenness,* the awareness of my own failures and shortcomings. When I'm aware of my own heart's condition, I'm far more humble and sensitive to a friend's struggle.

The path God often uses to draw me closer to Him is the path of brokenness and disappointment.[6] What I have to offer a friend never comes from a position of having arrived; it's rather a shared understanding that God works best in my weakness. I have difficulty relating to people with no admitted struggle.

In one of my many aborted attempts to right my capsizing financial ship, I agreed to meet with a financial counselor. I shared with him the issues we were facing, the mistakes I'd made, and what all of it did to my heart. As I finished my story, I asked if he'd ever struggled in this way. I was certain he would say he had. He quickly and confidently responded, "No." Perhaps he hadn't, but I left shortly after that, determined I wouldn't go back. I often wonder if this is how hurting people experience folks in our churches. They come with wounds, longing for understanding and healing, and are met by pious people who act like they have it all together.

When the Pharisees saw this, they asked his disciples, "Why does your teacher eat with tax collectors and 'sinners'?" On hearing this, Jesus said, "It is not the healthy who need a doctor, but the sick."[7]

We need to see friends through the eyes of our own brokenness.

The next stone we walk on is *boldness,* something that's especially needed as we live life at an incredible pace. Our schedules remind me of the teenagers' game decades ago of seeing how many could fit in a VW Beetle. We stay in constant motion, living in the car and on the cell phone and at the drive-through window. The message we send is, "You can be my friend if you can catch me."

As a result, many of us settle for acquaintances rather than friends. Our lives intersect at parties or in church lobbies. The conversation is pleasant and at times good. We leave longing for more. Then the alarm goes off signaling the start of the new day's race.

The boldness of friendship begins with the willingness to move into a friend's life amid the tyranny of such busyness.

This boldness is never arrogant. It's more than just the tenacity of finding time for someone; it's the humble but strong belief that I have something to offer you. What I have to offer is what God has placed in me through Christ Jesus. As a forgiven, redeemed child of God I can pour into the life of my friend something he or she needs not only to face life but to live it.

His divine power has given us everything we need for life
and godliness through our knowledge of him who called us
by his own glory and goodness.[8]

It's so hard to believe that truth. Our friends' marriage is ripping apart; we hope they find a marriage counselor. A teenager we know is dabbling in marijuana and Ecstasy; I call the youth pastor. The list goes on and on. We assume only experts can handle and heal the hurts. But God claims that He has placed *within us* all that we need for life.

When it comes to helping others live that life, I won't do it perfectly. I'm not an expert. I'm afraid I'll mess it up and embarrass myself. But let me tell you something I'm learning: There *are no* experts of the soul, but there *are* soul friends. And that's what we need.

The final stone that completes the path is *dependence.* Dependence on the Holy Spirit is essential if spiritual friendship is to develop. This stands in sharp contrast to the idea of having to "make it happen." I want to move into my friend's life with curiosity, brokenness, and boldness, but always listening to and relying on the prompting of the Spirit. This means I must always be willing to have *nothing* happen. The pressure's off. I don't need to always have an answer to life's questions and to fix the problem.

I recently had coffee with a friend. He shared a struggle he and his wife were having with their young son. He asked for my thoughts about the issues of control and fear as they related to his son's behavior; better understanding these issues would affect how they dealt with their son. I had no clear-cut insight about this, but I also felt no pressure to have it. My friend and his wife are good parents; they love their son. I'll continue to interact with my friend, and I'll pray and look for ways to pour into his life—perhaps with increasing wisdom as I engage more deeply with him.

JUST SHOW UP

The path of friendship isn't always a smooth, gentle walk. It's often messy. Friendships can be filled with annoyances. Therefore our responses need to be intentional. That process begins with a willingness to just show up. I don't know all that will be required of me, but I'm willing to enter even the uncertainty.

Friendship must be allowed to develop as life unfolds. It takes time, enough time for hope and patience to become real.

9

Living Authentically

It is in community that we learn to honor one another—to honor without flattery but with a love informed by truth. It is in community that we learn forgiveness—the capacity to bear with one another, as Christ has borne our sins and forgiven us.... It is in community that we love and receive love. Without community we remain fundamentally alone, one-dimensional and disconnected— not only from others but from ourselves and from God.

GORDON T. SMITH

On September 2, 2001, I lost control of my congregation. I couldn't grasp what was happening. Conversations would stop when I entered a room. Staff would turn their heads when they saw me approach. I felt as though people were avoiding me, and I didn't know why.

Twenty-five years of leadership, hard work, nurturing relationships, prayer, and giving of my life had led now to lies, deception, and shock. Actually, it was a wonderful day!

You're probably thinking, *This guy has lost it.* But before you put the book down and begin praying for my sanity, allow me to explain. That Sunday was the day our congregation surprised and honored Suzi and me for twenty-five years of ministry at Church at Charlotte. The staff and I had planned a worship service *they* knew would never take place. They even printed bogus bulletins. They allowed me to study and prepare, knowing full well I wasn't going to preach. I remember stopping several of them during the week and sharing some of what I planned to say on Sunday. They just smiled and said, "That sounds really good, Jim." They even got my mother to go along with the deception!

It was an extraordinary day. Suzi and I felt honored—so many people, so many kind words. For a long time I've felt privileged to pastor a unique group of people—that day helped to confirm the truth of what I felt.

The days that followed our surprise celebration were spent at an idyllic vacation spot. That gift of time away allowed us to reflect and soak in the goodness of all that had transpired. People had been encouraged to write notes of appreciation, and there was a mound of them to read. We read their words as if we were drinking cool water to quench our thirst. It was the refreshing water of God's love poured out through the lives of folks who have walked with us on the journey.

At the Heart of It

Reflecting on those letters stirred me to ponder the question, "What makes community at Church at Charlotte so unique, so important to me?"

I've had opportunities to speak around the country on the topic of community. Often I'm asked to describe our church community. What does it look like? In many ways we're no different from your church. We hold worship services and have Sunday school. We have programs for children, youth, men, women, singles, and married couples. We support missions, conduct outreach in our city…the list goes on. All are good endeavors, which we do with a desire for excellence, yet none of these efforts is at the heart of what brings about community.

What *is* at the heart? The answer is uncomfortably simple: Community involves people's lives intersecting one another and sharing in the life of Christ. What has made the Church at Charlotte so meaningful to me and to so many others is people's intentional movement into one another's lives. It's about people who have been released to bloom in their walk with God, people interacting within a theological foundation and in a framework that fosters connection at deep levels. I have the privilege to guide and nurture this community.

God's Word *must* be taught. It's foundational. Prayer *must* be encouraged. It's essential. Community, however, cannot be forgotten: It *must* be pursued. It's indispensable.

For early Christians, all three of these anchor points—the study of God's Word, prayer, and community—were part of the fabric of the church. As we've moved through time, churches have typically emphasized one of these at the expense of the others. But *all three need to be pursued.*

Deep, connecting, life-changing community is difficult to create and sustain, but we're doing it at our church. The movement has been intentional. I see it happening in small groups, in adult fellowships, and in one-on-one relationships. People are safely intersecting one another's lives, receiving and giving the life of Christ to each other.

The letters Suzi and I read on that anniversary getaway revealed a common thread that's woven into the fabric of our community—one that seems to enable this to happen:

- "Thank you for being real in a world where there are so many Christian leaders who hide behind a facade."
- "I enjoy your transparency as a fellow traveler who also struggles with life."
- "Thanks for teaching the Scripture in real and honest ways."
- "Thanks for living honestly. We love the genuineness of your heart."
- "You have not been afraid to become transparent to this congregation as you deal with life's circumstances."

While each person's story is different, this one value—transparent genuineness—seems to have helped each person experience acceptance and hope at the church. This core value, perhaps above any other, marks our ministry and helps make our community a safe place.

NEVER TELL?

Our commitment to be open and real was an intentional choice we made a long time ago.

In 1981, at age twenty-seven, I found myself at the church, without a pastor, and facing a crisis: We owed $28,000 (a debt left by our previous leadership), and it was due in just three weeks. The congregation numbered about one hundred, and those kinds of resources didn't exist. We were in deep trouble.

At the suggestion of a board member, Suzi and I sought the counsel of a well-known pastor. He was a respected speaker and leader who had more experience than any of us. He listened quietly while we painted our bleak picture, and when we finished, he paused, pushed back his coffee cup, and confidently announced, "Never tell your people where you're at."

"Excuse me?" I blurted out.

With a look of amazement, he responded, "Never tell them about financial trouble. If you have to get fourteen men to sign personal notes for $2,000 each, then do that—just don't let the people know. It will scare them away." I was so shocked that the only words I could muster were, "Thanks for your time."

The ride home was silent. As Suzi and I pulled into our driveway, I made it clear I couldn't lead that way. Regardless of the outcome, the people deserved the truth. Good or bad, we needed to be real, genuine, and authentic.

I believe an important value was established that night. No matter what, our community would be authentic. (By the way, we told the congregation the trouble we were in, and a week later took up a special offering that brought in more than $29,000—but that's another story.)

POINTING TO CHRIST

A safe community needs people committed to being authentic with one another, living as fellow strugglers in life's journey.

Paul brought out this truth: "But we have this treasure in jars of clay."[1] Fragile, flawed, breakable clay pots—we're all in that condition. Yet—and this is amazing—we possess the living Christ, in the person of the Holy Spirit, living in us. Divine "treasure" dwelling in ordinary humanity.

None of us, regardless of our place on the journey, has arrived. We never will. In a genuine gathering of believers, that truth needs not only to be known but to be readily expressed. Failing to do so, we'll likely set up a community based on deception, which will prevent our taking the next step.

For authenticity is not simply about creating a safe place where people are free to struggle. Paul finished his thought by writing that the reason we're clay jars is "to show that this all-surpassing power is from God and not from us."[2] This safe community, made up of authentic people who are all fellow strugglers on a journey, can live in such a way as to reveal the life-changing power of the gospel.

The point of being real and genuine is to point people to Christ. If we allow authenticity to become an end rather than a means, we create an environment that excuses behavior instead of celebrating the power of a life in Christ. The freedom authenticity brings allows me to place my confidence not in my performance, but in the work of Christ, as Paul did and taught:

> Such confidence as this is ours *in Christ....*

> Our competence comes from God. He has made us competent as ministers of a new covenant....

> Since we have such a hope [the reality of new covenant], we are very bold....

> God...always leads us in triumphal procession *in Christ.*[3]

As the church is released to function as a community, being authentic not only allows me to share my struggles but also helps me see the potential in others because of Christ. This, in turn, allows me to ponder how to stir them to love better and live to God's glory.

A young man who was broken and desperate came into our community several years ago. Choices he'd made in his life, as well as judgment pronounced on him by Pharisees in our city, had brought him to the point of hopelessness. He wondered if God could ever use him again. Our congregation provided a safe community that allowed healing to take place. In time, with accountability, love, and vision for his life, we restored him to service. But people outside our church went nuts. The now-familiar cries of "soft on sin" cascaded down and challenged our actions.

In the midst of this harsh reaction we saw the beautiful picture of a life-giving, life-restoring community. God's people stirred this young man to be released and transformed into Christ's likeness not because he was perfect but because of who Christ was in his life.

HOLD ON TO IT

I recently found a letter waiting for me in the kitchen when I came home from the church. Before I even opened the envelope, I knew what was inside. I would have to make a choice. It was an offer to become pastor at another church. To accept it would mean leaving a group of people who have been a part of my life for nearly three decades. It would also mean new challenges and opportunities. The size of the congregation was double our church, and there would undoubtedly be financial advantages as well.

As I scanned through the contents of the letter, I remembered a recent conversation with another pastor who'd left his church. "I've outgrown the congregation," he said matter-of-factly. Men and women in all walks of life make similar choices all the time. They leave one job to take another that promises more money and greater responsibilities, with the hope of moving them closer to their goal of personal satisfaction.

I looked back at the words in the letter. There was little doubt about what would be gained. Many would say it made sense…yet I said no.

Don't think of it, however, as some noble decision on my part. I declined the offer because of the community God placed me in, because of people I'm on a journey with—people who stir me and whom I stir to be released to shine the light of Jesus into our world. It was too much to give up.

When you find authentic community, hold on to it.

10

Living with Security and Passion

Man's chief end is to glorify God, and to enjoy Him forever.

THE WESTMINSTER CATECHISM

The New Way journey begins with a stunning revelation, not about us, but about God. The unapproachably holy, incomparably magnificent God wants us to enjoy Him, to actually come close and feel really good. He made us for the pleasure He enjoys when we enjoy Him.

LARRY CRABB

Jesus had the remarkable ability to cut through the complexity of life, pinpoint people's motives, and expose their heartbeat. More than once, He raised the simple question, "What do you want Me to do for you?" As the words hung in the air, those who listened were forced to examine what their hearts really wanted. The passion that drove their lives would be exposed before them and, often, before others.

One such incident involved James and John, who openly lobbied for positions of power and prominence. Their request ticked off the other disciples, in all likelihood because James and John had beaten them to the asking. The passion at the center of their world was to control life and to control others. Obtaining high-ranking spots in God's kingdom would be their ticket to ensure power.

One problem: The object of their passion wasn't even on the radar screen as far as Jesus was concerned. They had bought into a system the world espoused: The person at the top dictates life to those below. He sets the rules, he's in control, and whenever he's questioned he can simply reply, "Because I said so!"

But Jesus said, "If you follow me, you'll have to scrap the whole system. Greatness comes in serving others, and being top dog is learned only by being last in line." Okay, the exact quote is this:

> Not so with you. Instead, whoever wants to become great
> among you must be your servant, and whoever wants to be
> first must be slave of all.[1]

WHERE SECURITY BEGINS

To live in true community, as exemplified by Jesus, requires one to be a very secure person. In contrast, the world's system of power and control thrives on insecurity, even though the very nature of the system means that insecurity must remain hidden. Leaders who are insecure hide behind authoritarianism, knowing that the pecking order will be their salvation. They do not encourage people to grow or give them opportunities to use their gifts, for fear they might rise above and beyond current leadership.

In my early years of ministry I worked for a man who greatly controlled what I was allowed to do. He was a gifted but insecure teacher. Whenever I offered to handle the welcome and announcements in a worship service or lead the corporate prayer time, my offer was dismissed. He would do it all. In the four years we worked together, he allowed me to preach only once. It certainly couldn't have been the fear that I would preach better, yet the veil of control hid some sort of insecurity.

The path Jesus offers exposes insecurity and demands that people identify their passion as they serve others. If the church is to become a community, it will need people who are secure, free, and passionate.

Security begins with the recognition of who I am in Christ. "All this is from God, who reconciled us to himself through Christ."[2] God has made a new way of living available through His Son. My security, then, has nothing to do with my goodness or my abilities or my accomplishments. It's only because of what Christ has done.

How then does security affect the church community?

First, it allows me to relax and realize that I "belong." People long to know that they belong, that they are accepted. And as the truth of security in Christ is experienced, it begins to remove the significant question of belonging or not belonging.

Second, security tells me that all of us who know Christ are on an equal footing. He has accomplished for me the same realities that He has for you. We're equally forgiven, equally loved, equally His son or daughter. We're all important, we're all necessary to one another, and we all need one another. All of this delivers a sense of belonging because of what Christ has done.

As Ray Stedman wrote, "No one can properly think of himself as any closer to God, apart from Christ, than anyone else."[3]

Third, security frees me to live in new ways. Living in the reality of Christ's accomplishments and acceptance allows me to move beyond my own needs in order to serve others. As I'm convinced of what God has done for me, and as I experience His presence in my life, I'm able to open my heart and give to others. The security I experience becomes the fertile ground that produces unselfishness toward others.

To not have this freedom leaves me unable to move toward people. When I'm always wondering who will care for *my* needs and *my* concerns and follow *my* agenda, community is stifled. It all comes down to a question of whether I want to live with an insecurity and selfishness that looks out only for me or to thrive in a security that, because of Christ, enables me to move toward others.

WIDE OPEN HEARTS

In writing to the church at Corinth, Paul drew the conclusion that he had lived with an other-centered unselfishness toward them. After relating a long list of his experiences, from the worst of pain and hardships to the highest manifestations of virtue and joy, Paul noted that his actions had remained consistent:

> We have spoken freely to you, Corinthians, and opened wide our hearts to you. We are not withholding our affection from you.[4]

I'm also free to live with that wide-open-heart unselfishness toward others. It means I can take my hands off the controls and allow others to function. The insecure person says, "If I let someone else serve in my place, he might do a better job than I; then the church will decide they don't need me, and I could lose my position." Sometimes the reason for controlling behavior is as simple as wanting the spotlight for myself. To let others be recognized would mean less recognition for me, and that isn't acceptable. But someone who's secure is free to let others exercise their gifts. If they excel, then wonderful! The body of Christ is stronger as a result.

During one of the three sabbaticals I've been privileged to take over the years at the church, I learned something of giving up control. I missed our entire church budget-setting process while I was away. I remember telling a friend, a fellow pastor, about this. He was shocked. "Weren't you nervous?" he asked. "I could never let go like that."

But the process developed just fine without me, through capable elders and other staff. This experience freed me to understand that allowing others to use their gifts doesn't have to threaten my place in the body of Christ.

Living this way doesn't come naturally to us. Only the supernatural presence of the Holy Spirit makes it possible. "Where the Spirit of the Lord is, there is freedom."[5]

A PASSION FOR HIS GLORY

Out of that freedom and security, ordinary people living in community—convinced of what Christ has done and filled by the Spirit—are capable of living in a new way with a new passion. It's a passion that makes possible a lifestyle that explodes forth in the brilliant light of God's glory:

> And we, who with unveiled faces all reflect the Lord's glory, are
> being transformed into his likeness with ever-increasing glory.[6]

What an incredible possibility! You and I can live in a manner that reflects the very likeness of Christ. My passion for life can be more than *my* desires and *my* goals; it can be about reflecting Christ, revealing God.

All of this raises a very good question: What does it mean to live to the glory of God? Paul described the scope of life so that it covers everything:

> So whether you eat or drink or whatever you do, do it all
> for the glory of God.[7]

I can see that it's inclusive of all my life. His glory is to be evident in everything from routine choices to major decisions; but I'm still left pondering what it actually means to live for His glory.

The answer begins with the understanding that God's ultimate goal is to preserve His name and to display His awesome greatness.

> I will say to the north, "Give them up!"
>   and to the south, "Do not hold them back."
> Bring my sons from afar
>   and my daughters from the ends of the earth—
> everyone who is called by my name,
>   whom I created for my glory,
>   whom I formed and made.[8]

We were all created for God's glory. I'm to acknowledge Him above all, value Him above all, and make Him visible above all. I need to give Him my heart above all, trust Him above all, and love Him above all.

The key is found in the "above all." To live for His glory is to live in a way that reflects and reveals that I'm satisfied by Him and enjoy all that He is. We can honestly pray, "As I wrestle with the hunger You have given me for Yourself, help me settle for no other, lesser satisfaction."[9] When a community of believers lives with that kind of passion, the world will take notice! And it will help bring us through personal dark days and nights.

I stood with friends at the bedside of their eleven-year-old son as they watched him leave this world and be taken into God's presence. There were tears and questions and pain, all normal and legitimate. Yet as I stood there, I experienced a deeper and much quieter reality. I saw two people who hungered for the Lord and hoped in Him, and who were finding a storm-tossed peace in Christ. "Christ in you, the hope of glory"[10] took on flesh and bones. In the days that followed, doctors, nurses, and friends testified that something very unusual had taken place.

From the hardest times in life to the everyday activities, it's possible to live with a security-supported passion that points people to Christ, our true and only satisfaction in life.

Living with Humility

Your attitude should be the same as that of Christ Jesus:

Who, being in very nature God,

   did not consider equality with God something to be grasped,

but made himself nothing,....

   he humbled himself.

PHILIPPIANS 2:5-8

Sunday mornings have a familiar rhythm. I'm up, dressed, and out of the house before my family stirs. I stop at Starbucks on the way to church and buy four grande coffees, one for myself and three for worship team members who come early. I lock myself in my office, look over my notes, and spend time praying for the morning's events. Shortly after nine, I head over to the worship center and greet folks as they arrive for the early service.

One particular Sunday was no different until I saw a certain man slip into a back row. He was one of many visitors that day, but I recognized him as a man in ministry, well known and well traveled. I was also well acquainted with him. Our paths had crossed many times in ministry. Most of those occasions were unpleasant memories in my mind. He had made it clear that he had "arrived" and I had not. He had the answers; I did not. Any questions I asked were answered in a manner that clearly communicated his superiority. I was surprised to see him worshiping at our church. I went back to greet him, and we exchanged pleasantries.

As I turned to walk back to my seat, he made one final statement. "No need to introduce me this morning. I'm just a visitor." I nodded and moved on.

The service that morning produced very little worship for me. My head was spinning with so many other thoughts. "How could anyone think this way? Does he really believe he's that important? Why would I single him out over all the other visitors? How arrogant can a person be?"

A RARE TREAT

Perhaps the quality most absent in our Christian communities and our leadership is humility. Humility requires us to hold a correct vision of ourselves as sinners, to rely on what Christ has done, and to be others-centered.

When I was young and just beginning ministry, I attended as many pastors conferences as I could. I wanted to ask questions and learn from men whose experience and wisdom far exceeded my own. Often I left those conferences disappointed and disillusioned. Questions I asked were brushed aside as either trivial or naive. Personal encounters with these pastors left one thing very clear: *They* were important; *I* wasn't.

On one particular occasion I had the opportunity to meet a pastor of a very large church in a well-known denomination. The introduction went like this: "Dr. So-and-so, this is Jim Kallam, a young pastor in our area." I was wearing a sports coat that day with suede patches on the elbows. He looked at me and said, "Son, those patches need to be on your knees, not your elbows." He laughed, and those with him joined in. "You be sure and remember that," he added. Over twenty years later one thing is certain: I do remember feeling embarrassed and humiliated.

Humility is a rare treat. Encountering someone who possesses it feels like a refreshing breeze of cool mountain air on a hot day. One such person was the late Ray Stedman, pastor at Peninsula Bible Church in Palo Alto, California. I met Dr. Stedman at a time in his life when he'd already pastored more than thirty-five years at PBC. As you might have guessed, we met at a pastors conference.

I waited in line to speak to him. "Dr. Stedman, I'm a pastor, and I was wondering if I could ask you a couple of questions?" I nervously waited to see how he would respond. To my complete shock, he invited me back to his room and spent more than an hour not only answering my questions but asking me about my life and my ministry. I left that night struck by his openness, his warmth, and his humility. Here was a Christian leader who had "arrived" and who wasn't arrogant.

It's strange how such one-time encounters can leave powerful fragrances in our lives. Some are sweet-smelling aromas, and some just plain stink. Both kinds leave us facing the deepening reality that our lives have incredible capacity to impact others.

In community, the results can be even more profound. We need to understand humility; we need to be aware of the mark it will leave on those with whom we live in community.

Scripture makes it plain that God values humility as a character trait in His children:

Be completely humble and gentle.[1]

Do nothing out of selfish ambition or vain conceit, but in humility consider others better than yourselves.[2]

Clothe yourselves with compassion, kindness, humility, gentleness and patience.[3]

Remind the people...to be peaceable and considerate, and to show true humility toward all men.[4]

What exactly is this thing called humility that's so important to God?

Sitting with some friends the other day I asked, "How would you define humility? And who has shown you an example of it for you to model?"

We sat in silence for a long time. We know God values it. We long to demonstrate it in our lives. Yet humility remains elusive to define and difficult to understand. Having said that, allow me to take a stab at defining it.

A Correct Vision of Ourselves

Humility begins with modesty. Modesty is having an unassuming view of my value, abilities, achievements, and importance in the world. It involves seeing myself as small and, since I am small, it's a correct vision of myself. Humility is directed in two ways—toward God and toward others. When directed toward God, it includes the correct vision of myself that, as a sinner, I need to confess my sin. When I do, there's the deep realization of my unworthiness to receive His grace—and yet I have received it, because of Christ. To walk humbly with God is to gain a clear perspective on my relationship with Him and to live dependently in light of what Christ has done.

Humility directed toward God is best seen in my willingness to live in dependence on Him:

> He has showed you, O man, what is good.
>> And what does the LORD require of you?
> To act justly and to love mercy
>> and to walk humbly with your God.[5]

God desires to be the source of strength in whom we trust. He wants His people to rely on *Him* and not on what the world offers. The humble person is willing to do that.

When I begin to fathom the awesome love of God, I realize I have nowhere else to turn. But the arrogant person is blind to his need for God because he believes in himself. Arrogance is rejection of God—and it's dangerous:

> Woe to those who go down to Egypt for help,
>> who rely on horses,
> who trust in the multitude of their chariots
>> and in the great strength of their horsemen,
> but do not look to the Holy One of Israel,
>> or seek help from the LORD.[6]

When humility is directed toward others, it involves servant living for the good of another. Living humbly means pouring myself into others' lives, making their well-being a higher priority than my own. Many of my choices are made because they benefit me. They'll make my life easier, happier, more satisfying, or more complete. If, as I face those same choices, I respond believing the other person deserves the same consideration I seek, my decision will look different. In so demonstrating humility, I'm living out Hebrews 10:24.

THE ESSENTIALS OF HUMILITY

Two other words in Scripture are needed to complete the picture of humility: gentleness and meekness. Both are internal realities, graces of the Holy Spirit that shape a humble heart.

Gentleness has been defined as "the grace which pervades [my] whole nature, mellowing all which would have been harsh and austere."[7] This God-given quality brings about a change in who I am. Gentleness transforms a person with harsh, rough, and even crude edges into a person who's kind and useful toward others. A gentle spirit allows me to be used by God in building up others. This gentleness is not something I strive to produce; rather, it flows through me by the Spirit.

Meekness "does not denote outward expression of feeling, but an inward grace of the soul, calmness toward God."[8] In my relationship with God, I see how good His actions have been toward me, and that causes me to be at peace with Him. I'm able to rest in all that Christ has done for me.

Gentleness and meekness are essential to humility that clearly sees my place in community and lives dependently on God. So how will humble living impact my life and the life of the community? Humility impacts my life as I keep a clear perspective of who I am, both in relationship to God and to others. My awareness of my sinfulness keeps my perspective clear. It sounds strange, but it's true. My sin keeps me humble before God as I realize His amazing grace and my constant need for it. I'm also aware of His boundless love, a love that's so undeserved yet keeps flowing toward me.

In the book of James we're told, "Humble yourselves before the Lord, and he will lift you up."[9] I live with peace as I'm dependent on the Lord, knowing He's in control. In His time, He'll work His will in my life.

In my relationship to others, an awareness of my own sinfulness keeps a spirit of judgment from filling my soul. It's harder to be critical of others when I'm aware of my own failures. In addition, living humbly allows me to give to others in a manner that seeks their good. Humility provides the wisdom to know what's best for the community, instead of what's best for just me.

> When pride comes, then comes disgrace,
> but with humility comes wisdom.[10]

MY DAD

I mentioned earlier the two-part question I'd asked some friends about humility. In the silence that followed, I knew who it was who taught me the most about humility—my dad.

He was saved at an evangelistic crusade led by Mordecai Ham. (It happened to be the same crusade and the same night in which a young man by the name of Billy Graham accepted Christ as well.) In the decades since, my dad and mom have given their lives to ministry and to encouraging their children, blessing us with a godly heritage.

Dad has earned three master's degrees (music, arts, and divinity), and a Ph.D. Since our names are the same, I've kidded him and told him that when he no longer wants the degrees on his wall, I'll hang them in my office. His beautiful baritone voice has allowed him to sing all over the country, including on stage at the Metropolitan Opera.

In all these accomplishments, Dad has been to me a picture of humility. He has shown me by example what it is to be at peace with God. There's a calm about him that comes from knowing firsthand that God is good. Dad has lived with an unwavering dependence on the Lord. One of my strong memories is seeing him reading his Bible—he taught me to love God's Word. His humility also shows in how he treats others. I've watched over and over again as he has put others' interests ahead of his own.

Let me share one story. A certain young man is pastoring today who, humanly speaking, wouldn't be pastoring if it weren't for Dad. This young man was on the verge of being thrown out of Bible college. He was hardheaded and somewhat arrogant, but Dad saw something in him that was redeemable. So, although the college's administration was united in wanting to dismiss the young man, Dad risked his reputation as president of the college and wouldn't allow it. Many more stories like this are part of my memories of my dad living an others-centered life.

That's the kind of humility God longs for us to live out and the kind that helps community thrive.

Living with Strength

Church, a place where even the wild and wooly have grace.

Where we who don't have it all together,

come together once again.

The humble sit forgiven and speechless,

while the proud sit loudly and survey.

The half dead are fully alive, at least for a while,

and the half crazed are calmed once more.

We, in rare unity, lift up our hands and bow our hearts to worship God.

LISA KROONS

No trademark in the world is more recognizable than the Nike "swoosh." It appears at all kinds of sporting events and crosses all language barriers. Almost as famous as Nike's logo is their advertising phrase, "Just Do It." The words reflect the attitude of athletes on countless fields of competition: Use your talent, your ability, your determination, your drive...and you can accomplish your goal.

"Just Do It" works well in a sporting event, but not when it comes to living the Christian life.

STRENGTH IS ROOTED IN DEPENDENCE

Earlier we examined how our source of power is the Holy Spirit. His indwelling presence enables us to live a life that's in keeping with God's desire for us. The better way of the new covenant (see Hebrews 7:22) is realized only through the supernatural strength the Spirit provides. Unlike the individualism of "Just Do It" and the fierce independence of our culture, God says that strength is found in dependence.

David understood this truth:

> To you I call, O LORD my Rock;...

> The LORD is my strength and my shield;
>> my heart trusts in him, and I am helped....

> The LORD is the strength of his people.[1]

David was trusting God as the source of stability—his rock. He saw God as his place of shelter—his shield. He regarded Him as someone he could depend upon for all that was lacking in his own life. God was David's source of strength. And God desires to provide us that same strength.

Paul hinted at a paradox when he talked about strength in weakness. He wrote in 1 Corinthians that it's the "weak things of the world [that] shame the strong."[2] Therefore we can't boast or somehow believe that our accomplishments are our own doing. Later, in 2 Corinthians, Paul referred to his own struggles and once again pointed to the source of strength as being supernatural:

> Therefore I will boast all the more gladly about my weak-
> nesses, so that Christ's power may rest on me.[3]

Living with strength begins with the realization that the Christian life cannot be lived as God intended apart from the Holy Spirit. "Just Do It" will be accomplished only as the supernatural life of Christ is released in my being.

That's why we need to value our relationship with the Holy Spirit as being more important than the methodology we follow. We must embrace the mysterious and not seek to reduce everything to formulas.

What would individuals living in that kind of strength look like as a community? How would God's kingdom be lived out?

> By showing to others the presence of the kingdom in the
> concrete details of our shared existence, we impact the lives
> and hearts of our hearers, not just their heads. And they
> don't have to write it down to hold onto it.[4]

Strong community life is a compelling model and example of God working in us as two realities become visible: We take on the life of a servant, and we encourage others to be empowered to serve.

EMPOWERED TO SERVE

We see ourselves in interesting ways. Winston Churchill once said, "We are all worms. But I do believe I am a glowworm." Muhammad Ali declared himself to be the greatest. How many of us see ourselves as servants? But that's what God chooses to call us.

True strength, by God's definition, is seen in the willingness to serve. Serving is the desire to be of help to someone, with no thought of personal gain or recognition. Strong communities are those where people see themselves as called to serve one another, where hearts are filled with the Spirit and bathed in love.

People who are convinced that God will meet their needs are free to be committed to live for the well-being of others. Their mind-set is that life isn't just about "me, myself, and I"; there's a larger story being told by God.

It sounds so simple, but it's not, because my sin nature competes against this attitude of service. I have a built-in preoccupation with my own significance. When my pride is released, it wrecks community. Pride, the oldest sin in the world, is still the most dominant, and it wears many faces.

Pride is seen in vanity, when my appearance and how others view me becomes an all-consuming concern. It's seen in my stubbornness, my desire to have things my way. And it's seen in exclusion, the belief that I don't need you. All these struggles are very real and work against my living as a servant.

Strength is found in releasing the Spirit-driven ability to live for others. I need to understand that this is more fundamental to who I am than my selfish need for attention. Jesus called the disciples to follow Him, to follow His example of service. He modeled biblical servanthood as an antidote to the values of a narcissistic world. Serving becomes the platform from which I care for others.

So many images flash in my mind that illustrate this truth, images I've witnessed in our community:

- A man is doing dishes after a church dinner. I discover later he's a leading surgeon in our city.
- A businessman leaves work and gives his time to an inner-city ministry by counseling families about their finances.
- A family leaves the warmth of their home on Christmas and serves a meal to the homeless.
- A group of retired men give one day every week to fix things around the church. (They also drink a lot of coffee.)
- A woman who has had four family members die of cancer drives cancer patients to their doctors' appointments.
- A husband and wife use money they've inherited to pay hospital bills for Suzi when they discover she's pregnant and we have no insurance.
- A woman invites people without family to join her family during the holidays.

Most people don't know about these acts of service. But then, serving isn't about recognition; it's about showing the kingdom of Christ to someone by helping them.

Encouraging others like this should be a rhythm of life. "There is perhaps no more powerful ministry that we can have to one another than the ministry of encouragement."[5]

SPIRITUAL GIFTING

Spiritual gifts play a vital role in the community's serving one another. Three words sum up what's essential for this to take place: *inform, encourage,* and *release.*

People need to know that they've been gifted by the Spirit: "Now to each one the manifestation of the Spirit is given."[6] They must understand that just as people are different, so are the gifts: "We have different gifts."[7] My own God-given gifts aren't for my benefit, but for the good of the community: "So that the body of Christ may be built up...attaining to the whole measure of the fullness of Christ."[8]

Encouragement happens when you and I realize that the community, the body of Christ, will be handicapped unless we contribute and serve. "But in fact God has arranged the parts in the body, every one of them, just as he wanted them to be."[9] Paul's wonderful analogy to the human body is encouraging—every part is needed, and no part can exist without the remaining parts.

As people are informed and encouraged, they need to be released—to be given permission to serve. And as they're turned loose and cheered on, their community will take on a quality of life that's contagious.

Eyes Fixed on Jesus

When we become followers of Christ, we become members of His church—and our commitment to the church is indistinguishable from our commitment to him. Radical words.... Yet according to the Scriptures, Christianity is corporate.

CHARLES COLSON

I love the church. I know it's flawed and that many times the experience of going to church leaves people disillusioned and frustrated. But I love the church. God loves the church. He has a passion for the church. And to this unique group of individuals that He has called into relationship with Him, He has also given the ability to thrive in relationship with each other.

You may be Baptist, Presbyterian, independent, Episcopal, or Evangelical Free—it doesn't matter. Your church may be large or small, rural or urban—the message stays the same. God wants your church released to become a community. You might be a pastor, a small-group leader, a Sunday-school teacher, or simply someone who cares deeply and prays accordingly for your congregation. The challenge goes out, no matter what your role: You can arouse a passion in others to love better and to live better for Christ. It *is* possible!

In our fragmented and disconnected world, Christ is calling us to reflect and reveal His life-changing message. It's a message He has given to the church. It's a message that's seen in a loving community:

> A new command I give you: Love one another. As I have
> loved you, so you must love one another. By this all men
> will know that you are my disciples, if you love one another.[1]

What an amazing concept. The world will realize that I follow Jesus by how I treat others who follow Him. That list includes my wife, my daughters, the elders in our church, and even people with whom I struggle to get along. I'm called to love them.

Church isn't a call to a frenetic schedule of activities, but rather a call to meaningful engagement in the lives of other believers. When the author of Hebrews exhorts us, "Let us not give up meeting together,"[2] it's a rich concept that goes way beyond using guilt to leverage folks to make it to a church service. Church, in the truest sense, requires powerful involvement with one another, and it cannot take place if we discontinue corporate worship, common fellowship, and continual relationship. To do so would be fatal to our walk with Christ. We're called to point people to Christ, a relationship that requires community. As the writer to the Hebrews said, "Let us fix our eyes on Jesus."[3]

If we lose sight of Jesus, we'll grow weary and lose heart.[4] The failure to see Christ, which is a direct result of the absence of community, brings consequences that are powerful in their destructiveness.

Growing Weary

As I grow weary—not just physically but also emotionally and spiritually—I become susceptible to making mistakes. I open myself up to doing foolish things, to making poor choices. The struggle of the Christian life becomes a draining experience as I fight life's daily battles. I become tired. Christ, speaking through Peter, called us to live in this world as aliens and strangers: "Dear friends, I urge you, as aliens and strangers in the world, to abstain from sinful desires, which war against your soul."[5] But as we battle life in the way Peter described, a powerful and damaging thought process can take control within us.

"What difference does it make how I live?" we ask. "No one cares what I do. When's the last time my life made a difference to anybody else? I should go ahead and indulge myself. I *deserve* it. God doesn't really care. If He did, He wouldn't have made life so hard and unfair."

I need a community to steer me away from such thinking and to point me to Christ—to encourage me to not grow weary or live foolishly.

Losing Heart

The other damaging consequence of taking my focus off Jesus is to "lose heart," to give up. It brings a crisis of faith.

I was recently talking with a friend about some trying times he was facing. He'd lost his job, his wife had filed for divorce, and his church had shunned him as a result. What a contrast to how he'd grown up. He trusted Christ at a young age, and during his high school and college years he was on fire for Christ. He seemed to always be sharing his faith, going on summer mission trips, leading Bible studies, and volunteering at church. Now, as we talked, all of that was a distant memory. He was making lifestyle choices that raised concerns.

As we talked about these choices, he shrugged his shoulders and turned away from my gaze. As we parted, his final statement was blunt: "It just isn't worth it anymore. If this is what following Christ gets you, I want no part of it!"

I left saddened and with a chill running down my spine. Where was a loving community to point him to Christ?

Those are tough times. I know their difficulty in part because I've experienced them personally. Pastors and missionaries and the like—those who fill the role of shepherding God's church—are people who struggle. Like anyone else, at times we wonder where God is, what He is or isn't doing. We can—and do—take our eyes off Jesus. When that happens, we're left weary and we lose heart.

Chuck Swindoll speaks of the emptiness of soul he encountered in the life of one pastor.

> This was the cry of one clergyman who whispered to me
> following a meeting with pastors, "Nobody around me
> knows this, but I'm operating on fumes. I am lonely, hol-
> low, shallow, enslaved to a schedule that never lets up."
> As I embraced him and affirmed his vulnerability and
> honesty, he began to weep with deep, heaving sobs. We
> prayed before he slipped back into the crowd.[6]

We pastors need community just as much as the people we shepherd.

When I was installed as pastor, the speaker for the installment service was the man who had been my pastor when I was growing up. I was so young and inexperienced; he was the wise, seasoned veteran who had been in the trenches, fought the battles, and had the scars to show as proof. Suzi and I hadn't had a pastoral mentor, so at dinner that weekend we decided to glean from this experienced husband and his wife. We asked this question: "If you could offer only one piece of advice as we begin ministry, what would it be?"

Many years later I can still hear his voice thunder in my mind: "Don't *ever* have friends from within your congregation." His wife emphatically nodded her head in agreement.

We never followed their advice. Instead, our friends have come out of our community. We know that our needs are no different from those of the people I pastor. If I proclaim that community is vital, then I must be willing to live it as well.

COMPELLED BY LOVE

So what inspires the kind of loving community that can make a difference in people's lives? As I consider—as I think hard—how to stir a passion in another believer to walk with Christ, I wonder: What will sustain my desire to impact them in this way? And what will allow them to receive my prompting?

As I ponder these questions, my mind is drawn back to John, the disciple Christ loved. His writing leaves little doubt that he had an undeniable interest in knowing and understanding love. The topic is synonymous not only with his gospel writings but also with his letters to the church. John could see the unbreakable connection between God, who is love, and our ability to love one another. And as we love one another, the result is stunning: The invisible God will actually be *seen*.

> No one has ever seen God; but if we love one another, God
> lives in us and his love is made complete in us.[7]

This is the picture: Men and women who are powerfully grounded in God's love, and who have experienced an inward healing as a result of that love, are transformed in a way that allows love to be expressed within community.

The generous, gracious, and forgiving love of God is the catalyst that allows us to love in that way. It's the answer to the question, "If God has devoted Himself to us with such an exhaustive and complete love, what choice do I have but to love?" There is no choice; I *must* love. Such love isn't produced by fear or guilt or by law. Instead Christ's love compels us to love.[8] "Whenever our perception of God is shaped by fear and anxiety, worry perhaps over losing his affection, we have not plumbed the depth of his love. We have not experienced his commitment to us."[9]

Loving communities take shape in an atmosphere of safety, vision, wisdom, and power. They're created by people who have a passion to celebrate grace, who envision potential, who discern and remove obstacles, and who long to enable others to bloom out of knowing God's incredible love for them.

Listen again to the apostle John:

> Dear friends, since God so loved us, we also ought to love
> one another.[10]

We're built for that kind of community. I can't get too much of it. Neither can you.

But How?

By now you may be saying, "This is good news. Yes, I want to experience this in our church, our small group. So tell us how! Get practical and show us what to do!"

Here's where I disappoint you. I'm not going to tell you how. Go ahead, put the book down, yell, scream, get frustrated. Then let me explain why.

There isn't only one way to have a loving community. Every leader is different; so is each congregation. Community is about being, not doing. It's about people relating, not programs functioning. It's found in understanding what Christ has accomplished and seeing it released in my life and yours.

I've sought to communicate in these chapters the ingredients necessary to build community. My desire is that you will take them and go build your community.

Have a blast! Laugh, cry, think hard, and pray. Discover that church, when released, *is* important.

PART FOUR

Stories of Community

For thirteen chapters you've listened to my story and my beliefs about community. These beliefs form a theological framework and provide a foundation that allow the church to be released and community to be lived out. This community is where lives intersect and people are pointed toward Christ, where the life of Christ is revealed and released in people, and where Christ is glorified and made visible. I believe community is important and necessary for growth in our walk with Christ. Many in my community share this belief.

I want to introduce you to four people who have experienced community at our church. While each story is different, the conclusions are the same: God uses community to stimulate growth and transformation in people's lives.

These are just four stories. Many more pictures of community cover the landscape of our church. You'll find their stories being lived out every day, in times of tragedy as well as in good times.

One of my greatest thrills as a pastor is to observe these tangible expressions of community lived out. Through these four stories, allow me to share my joy and encourage you to envision what can be.

A Story of Hope

Bill and Tamea Bock's story covers a difficult time in their lives. During their son William's battle with leukemia and his subsequent death, they were given a picture of community. It's a picture of loving support as the community struggled together to find hope in the midst of heartache.

=≡◁0▷≡=

O ften church is a place for casual conversations, friendly support, and catching up with the lives of our weekly acquaintances. Sometimes it's a much more meaningful place.

We found out just how important our church community could be when our nine-year-old son, William, was diagnosed with leukemia. We experienced the natural responses of friends and neighbors who reached out and lent a hand, made a meal, picked up our other kids at school. But for a single young woman to leave her apartment and live in our house for three months while we moved to another city to get William a bone marrow transplant is special. For a church body to organize a twenty-four-hour prayer vigil is special. For a church family to organize a blood drive to replace the dozens of units of blood our son received is special. For a congregation to organize scheduled prayer times during the day for weeks on end is special. It was simply more than many people would do for another.

Life can feel very lonely when the rest of the world seems to be getting along just fine while your life is absolutely falling apart. The usual clichés offered to those who are hurting just aren't enough when your child may be dying. It takes people of courage and compassion to get involved with their hearts to see how they can really help—not only with the logistics of dealing with an illness or injury but also to help you understand your anger at God, your fears and doubts. Not many want to go there. It's risky, and often the answers aren't clearly available.

Bold, Creative Caring

I remember meeting a friend at an ice cream shop while we took a needed break from the hospital. He asked the usual questions about my son's situation, but then pursued my heart by asking, "How are you doing with God in all of this?" I told him that if my son were cured, it would be easy to be His biggest supporter, a devout spokesman for the Lord and His healing power. But if my son didn't make it—who knows? I wasn't sure where that road would take us. My friend was brave enough to ask a hard question and really listen to the answer I gave.

On another occasion, after receiving traumatic news regarding our son's illness, a friend who coordinated many of the efforts on our behalf sat on the kitchen floor and cried with my wife. They both ended up practically under the kitchen table as they deeply grieved the reality of William's imminent death.

Several key friends walked this journey with us more closely than others, but we always felt the whole church community was with us in spirit and in prayer.

During William's illness we began sending e-mails to keep friends and family aware of the latest developments. This quickly became a vital outlet in the form of a personal journal that allowed us to express our thoughts and ideas as we traveled along this road. We talked about things William said and did, our own hopes and fears, the theological points we wrestled with, even helpful books that we'd read. Our list of e-mail recipients, dubbed "William's Army," grew to about eighty persons. Through this we recruited a huge prayer network and later met dozens of good people who were praying for us.

As I look back now, I realize just how many people performed amazing acts of love. The most effective helpers didn't just ask, "What can we do to help?" but rather took action. With the organizational oversight of a close friend who knew our particular needs, they brought lunch to the hospital, went Christmas shopping for us, planted pansies in our flower beds, cared for our dog, and spent time with our two daughters. All of this was coordinated so that we were confronted with very few decisions. Our ability to think about daily things and be gracious was at a minimum, so others did it for us. We learned from them how to care for others in creative ways. These folks heard the call of Jesus and responded. They allowed us to focus entirely on the health of our son and the well-being of our family.

And the love never stopped. After William's death, people continued to work behind the scenes in quiet, powerful ways. A lovely playground was erected in our son's memory with many folks volunteering their time and services. We now have a tangible memorial for other children to enjoy.

Because others did so much of the "stuff of life" for us, we were freed up to carry on a degree of normal life with our girls, while at the same time we began processing the painful loss of our son. We were able to do the work of grief that required so much physical and emotional energy, and at the same time begin to re-create our family, one that would never be the same. Without a doubt, much of the healing and wholeness we experience today, even in the ongoing pain, can be attributed to the *long-term* care we received from our church community.

Presented with Truth

Those who were involved even more intimately allowed us to express fear, anger at God, and concerns about heaven. We felt tremendous support from our small group—four couples who served as compassionate partners in this journey. We were concerned about the status of our marriage as well, so we pursued counseling to help us understand the different ways we handle stress and grief. Knowing that many marriages don't survive the loss of a child, we sought and found a counselor who helped us avoid yet another tragedy in our family. He and our pastor made numerous trips—several hours away—just to visit, check on us, and be present when big events in William's treatment took place. They cleared their calendars to walk willingly into a place of tragedy. Even as we held William for the last time, during his last breaths and final heartbeat, these two friends and another from our small group joined us in singing the doxology and ushering him into heaven. They poured themselves out for us.

When we were at a particularly low point in our relationship after William's death, we arranged to meet with our pastor, some members of our small group, and our counselor. Our pastor's wife graciously invited us all to their home for dinner. We felt so completely surrounded by love as we sat in their den and expressed our frustrations and disappointment with each other and with life in a fallen world. These caring servants listened intently to us and then gently helped us understand where we were going astray. They directed us to Him, indirectly, but with great power. That evening will always be treasured as a turning point in our journey. They presented us with Truth, without trying to provide simplistic biblical answers to our needs.

And while our friends' wisdom and love for us were great, their support didn't replace our need for Christ and the hope of heaven. More than anything, it pointed us to Him and eternity. For although we may have felt abandoned by Him at times, we were constantly being shown His concrete love at every turn. It's difficult to turn away from One who gives so lavishly. We recoil when people comment on our strength, faith in the midst of trial, and so on, knowing that the choice to follow Him was made so simple because we were shown His love so well.

One of the things we look forward to in heaven is the joy of living in community…community in its highest form, worshiping the One who modeled how to pour out our lives for one another. We've tasted deep love from the heart and can hardly wait for more![1]

15

A Story of Growth

Dave Joffe is a businessman who came to Church at Charlotte sixteen years ago along with his wife, Terri, when they were a young couple. For Dave, a new believer, it was his first experience in a church. The process of his understanding and seeing the power of community has been a slow one, often bathed in skepticism. Still, community holds a powerful place today in Dave's life.

—=≍≍≡◉≡≍≍=—

J im Kallam has prodded our congregation toward several goals over the past few years. He presents the goals each year in the form of a vision he has for the church. The goals have included our gaining the understanding that Christ is "on the move," that He's being formed in us, that our hearts are being transformed, and that we can now live with excellence.

Jim is consistent in stressing that we hear these topics as a community, not just as individuals. I think of hearing as an individual as receiving knowledge. On the other hand, I think of applying what we hear in our community as wisdom. It's this wisdom I've gained, albeit small, that I want to discuss here.

After I married my wife, Terri, it wasn't too long before I realized I was in a small community. There were now two of us where there had been one of me. I would say that our becoming "one flesh" resembled more of a skin graft than a smooth beautiful union. Through the guidance of the Holy Spirit, though, we've come a long way. I adore her. If you met her, you would see why. Each of our three children is uniquely amazing as well. God has given each of us strengths and weaknesses that make our family a wonderful place to be and enjoy. Jim's discussion about community includes this, but has forced me beyond these borders to a new, uncharted territory—to the men in my church, and beyond.

PLAYING THE GAME

I started in a small group at our church sixteen years ago. I've been consistently involved in small groups ever since. Until the last two years, I've observed that these groups are places for us to "play" community. I remember one of these groups through two images. In the first, I can see one of the members of our group, Brent, telling us about his week: His wife and two girls were doing well, but his job at a market research firm was tenuous. I fast-forward to the second image: He's thirty pounds lighter, hair slicked back, glasses shed, living with a woman whom he met on the Internet.

Why didn't he tell us back then that he found his wife unattractive? Why couldn't he tell us of his budding romance in cyberspace? He was only "playing" community. We couldn't encourage him to love and good deeds because we didn't know his struggles. I tried to change these superficial relationships to no avail. I heard the message clearly: Community is to be played, not lived. The Christian walk is a game to be played, not a life to be lived.

As Jim challenged us to be a part of authentic community, specifically through small-group experiences, my view of the challenge was jaded. I feared further rejection if I brought up something substantive. I feared failing at the game I was supposed to play. I didn't know whether the emotional investment would be worth the return in relationships and Christian maturity. As I've learned to do, I prayed for my sin to be uncovered, especially the sin that kept me from this community directive that's so clear in the Scriptures. I also prayed to be changed, through the Holy Spirit, so I could have the perseverance and endurance to meet the challenge, if it would further God's kingdom.

Finally I joined a small group of men who met during the workweek. After six months, I felt the same about this group as I had about those in the past. All the men were "playing" community. Any time one of us would try to speak about life in an honest way, the group would ignore that person. We felt like fools if we brought up a struggle or even a joy, for that matter. We wanted to display our knowledge and achievements rather than express our doubts, fears, or failures. One guy in the group, Ernie, said it best: "I don't like to do things where I don't look like I have my act together."

Amen. He'd finally stated the cardinal rule of men's small groups: Discussions should be limited to topics that allow the participants to appear to have their acts together. The topics should allow everyone to display appropriate levels of humor, intelligence, and general bravado. I concluded, sarcastically, that Jesus died on the cross so we could appear to be perfect. But I could not participate in that. I wasn't perfect and didn't even appear to be perfect. I told the group leader that I hoped he wouldn't be offended if I bowed out of the group but that I found it to be much too oppressive and stressful. He asked me to stick with it just a bit longer.

Chinks in the Armor

After a while, I noticed chinks in some of the men's armor. One of the guys in the group, Al, is a successful business executive. I've seen him in action. Prior to meeting him in the group, I thought of him as a man driven toward business goals. In the group, however, he discussed his wife, his kids, and the death of his father. He cried about his father's final days and his salvation on his deathbed. He's new to the depths of Christianity. The movement of the Holy Spirit in his life touched me. Where was the tough business zealot? Why was this goal-driven, fact-oriented thinker expressing feelings? I was learning about life.

Another man in our group, Brian, is intensely intelligent, especially in spiritual topics, church history, and apologetics. I never understood his intensity and found it intimidating. One day he discussed his dreams of being a missionary. He also discussed how he'd put away those dreams for the responsibilities of being a husband and a father. I saw that his intensity was just an ember of a deeper fire inside of him that was all but quenched. I understood how this created strains in his soul.

Most influential were the discoveries that I made about myself. One day I was having lunch with another member of the group. Fred had a history of problems dealing with money. He told me about how he had grown up in an affluent area, but he wasn't affluent. He told me about going to a birthday party as a youngster in a limousine with his friend from school. He had decided that neither he nor his family were going to be denied those things, regardless of his means.

I told him that I, too, had grown up in an affluent area but in a family that wasn't affluent. I took the opposite direction, however; I hoarded money as a defense against those "mean, arrogant" rich people. I wouldn't let go of that money even if I had the means to spend it. (I failed to mention earlier that the mean income of our small group is probably several times that of an average U.S. family. No wonder I was so stressed! What was I doing hanging around a bunch of rich guys? Yet why were they so much like me? Could I continue to put up a barrier?)

At this point, I dropped my defenses. I figured that the barriers I'd put up were the result of irrational views of life that I'd developed. I also concluded that any pain that came from dropping those barriers could be counted as sacrifice for the cross. My "us versus them" view was being debunked.

OUT OF HIDING

If anyone in the group was clearly "them," it was Charlie. Charlie is a gregarious person. When you first meet him, he seems very friendly. After a few meetings, however, you notice insecurities and competitiveness. The leader encouraged each of us to "tell our stories." Charlie's story was compelling. He'd endured unmitigated insults from his father from a very early age. He had never finished college and felt inadequate. His insecurity and competitiveness were understandable after he told us about himself. How could I reject someone who himself had been rejected so long?

One of the other guys, Kent, is very intense. I admired his openness more than anyone else in the group, but it scared me. He would discuss any topic at the drop of a hat, including intimate thoughts or arguments with his wife and children. When he told his story, we saw a childhood filled with drunken parents and weekends scarred by neglect. Seeing the image of him crying himself to sleep each weekend night as his parents were passed out from a drunken binge, I could accept his intensity. It was a necessary reaction to his intensely painful upbringing.

Keep in mind that all these men are quite successful. None of these issues gets in the way of their seeming ability to master life. In fact, I'm bold enough to think that you, too, are around people with very real stories like these, and you don't even know it. How can we grow in Christ when such darkness and, sometimes, light are hidden from His body?

My Turn

Then came my turn to tell my story. I included the points in my life that have shaped me into who I am. Unexpectedly, I cried as I told it. I cried intensely, as a matter of fact. When I looked up, I saw three of the men—Ernie, Dave, and Jerry—crying with me. Unless my experience deceives me, I think these men truly care about me.

As a Jew, as well as a believer in Jesus, I've rarely trusted outsiders. I've heard stories about what people are capable of doing to other people. My lack of trust and faith was now being debunked. After a good hearty cry, Ernie said he was exhausted from crying, and it was my life that exhausted him! I care for these men.

After all these experiences, feeling is returning to my soul like sensation returning to a crippled appendage. I'm starting to understand why we behave the way we do. On a men's retreat I found myself with a group of men, many I didn't know, who were being entreated to care for one another. Once again, I didn't feel much for this group with whom I had little in common. I prayed for my heart to be opened so I could care for those around me.

During a break, I was cleaning a coffee pot when a man came up to me. I'd seen Larry crying during one of the prayer times. I knew he had a son who had been diagnosed with muscular dystrophy. He told me how he couldn't understand God. He shared how hurt he was by life. I listened and felt compassion for him. I had no answers, but I cared. I pray that my continued caring will help him as he endures hardships in the kingdom of God.

I've come to learn that I can be sensitive to people who don't express their struggles and joys well. One of my friends, Peter, is very quiet. One day at church, he mentioned in jest that he knew we would enjoy watching the Coca-Cola 600 that weekend. Being from Charlotte, I've committed cultural heresy in never having been to a NASCAR event. I enjoy Peter, however, and I mentioned to my family that we should drop in on him and watch the race on his wide-screen television. He even equipped me with a Mark Martin "Viagra" hat, and I was a full-fledged race fan for the night. Jimmy Johnson was very effective that day, but Mark Martin won. So did Peter and I. He later sent a note saying he'd always wished someone would "drop in on him" and share an experience like this with him.

These experiences have informed me that I can contribute my gifts to our community and that others can contribute to me. Most notably, I've noticed that others can see my weaknesses and strengths better than I can. Self-deception and rationalization seem to be chronic symptoms of our sin condition. One of my friends, Dave, confronted me about my not wanting to buy a new house for our family. I thought I handily defended my position with my rationalizations about debt-free living. He countered that my hoarding tendencies were pushing me toward relative neglect of my family in that I could well afford a bigger house. He was right.

He also has confronted me about the nature of my gifts. He made me realize that I was not using my strongest gifts, the gifts of insight and discernment, in my life. At the same time, my boss, Steve, saw the same gap between my gifts and my vocation. Both of these men encouraged me to make a career change, at forty years old. There's little chance this would have happened had they not cared enough to know me and tell me their vision for me. I've tried to pass this kind of encouragement on to others.

BEYOND THE CHURCH

I've come to realize that the dynamics of community can extend beyond our local church. I have a new boss, Tom. Recently, his wife gave birth to a baby with Down's syndrome. In the past, I would have avoided discussing this because I had no answers. I would fear saying the wrong thing or offending him. Now I know that it means a lot to him that I care. I don't need to have answers. Each day, I pray for him. I write him notes telling him of my prayers. His response has been surprising.

One day Tom called me and told me he thought that one aspect of my work was more of a hobby than a part of my job. (Remember that I'm pursuing a new career, so my steps are tenuous.) When we discussed one of the deliverables that I'd produced, he told me (in much stronger terms than I can write here) that he thought my thesis wasn't true. This caused me to put up my old barriers and harbor anger. I prayed to God to judge between us, and I asked Him for help with my fantasy life. I often enjoy tearing someone down verbally in my own mind. Unfortunately, God views this as a sin, regardless of whether it took place only in my mind.

At the same time, our project came under scrutiny, and one of my colleagues told me that my boss, Tom, might not be on the project for the long-haul. Now I had two issues that posed a problem: I'm mad at Tom, and he may be moved off of the project. Should I tell him? My barriers were up. I asked my old boss, Steve, for advice. He told me I should tell Tom all of this if he's a friend, and avoid it all if our relationship is just professional. I heeded that advice.

Tom came into town a week later, and I felt compelled to tell him about my anger and also about the potential changes in our organization. His first words were, "You can't hurt me." I thought he was going to start discussing his super-strength and how other people cannot hurt him. To my surprise, he told me I couldn't hurt him because I'm his friend. He also said he considers me a fellow believer and that I, of all people, shouldn't let the sun go down on my anger. He said I should have called him at home and confronted the issues. He said that he was surprised I would be silent "after all that we've been through."

I've known Tom for only eight months, but I think my prayers and caring through the birth of his child have bonded us in a way that I didn't understand. He, like all of us, has enjoyed being known and cared for.

These experiences have extended to many other relationships outside of my church, to both believers and nonbelievers. I pray it continues. I've learned to face my doubts, fears, and failures as I grow in Christ as part of a community. The idea of a caring community isn't dead and need not be a farce. I pray for endurance to continue in this work of the kingdom of God.

16

A Story of Restoration

The next story involves repentance and restoration. It's a story of redemption, a picture of God's redeeming love. Out of respect for their privacy and a desire to avoid unnecessary hurt, the folks involved will be nameless. None of that diminishes this picture of God's grace and the role community has played in providing healing.

━━◄══◄ ◦◉◦ ►══► ━━

I would like to tell you of my journey through a dark canyon of my life. It was a journey filled with pain and sorrow, largely for my closest loved ones; it was a dark time in my life that would ultimately open many opportunities to learn of God's incredible love—as my community, my wife, and my family and friends taught me about love, grace, and forgiveness.

Sad to say, we often have to lose something very special before we learn to appreciate it. Fortunately this time, God provided a unique opportunity of restoration with my wife, my family, and my circle of friends— my community.

WALKING AWAY

I came to know Christ as Lord and Savior in my early twenties. God quickly put a loving community around me. (I must admit that at this point I knew very little about community—what it meant and how it could be such an incredible part of my life.) I was surrounded by mature Christians, men and women in pursuit of God. This was an exciting time of teaching, training, and learning God's Word. During this time I developed many close friends and met the woman who would ultimately become my wife and who today is my best friend.

Within three years of marriage, God moved us to a new job in a different part of the country and provided a new circle of friends. He blessed us with our first child, a gift from Him. A short time later, a second child whom we loved dearly was born. Then, after many years, we had a third beautiful baby whom we adored. Our lives were blessed beyond our imagination. Not only did our family increase in size, but our circle of friends did too. We continued to grow in our spiritual lives as our Christian community grew around us.

On the outside, life would appear nearly perfect. What else could a man ask for? I had a beautiful wife, three wonderful and healthy children, a good job, and a community of great friends. People often referred to us as the all-American family. Beneath the surface, however, things were not as they seemed.

Throughout the first eighteen years of our marriage, my own selfish and introverted personality, fueled by low self-esteem and difficult issues, caused me to slowly pull away from my community, especially my wife. With a heavy business travel schedule and quiet, unanswered inner needs, I began looking for my personal satisfaction outside my marriage rather than seeking answers from my wife or my circle of friends. At a point when my wife's family was in disarray, I thought I had justifiable excuses to walk away from everything. I left my entire Christian community behind. I betrayed my wife, my family, my friends, and most important, my God.

REACTIONS

When I walked away, my community responded in several different ways. Some individuals took what I would call a truth-only approach toward me. They very quickly pointed out my sin (something that deep within my soul I was fully aware of), then refused to associate with me. In some cases they chose not to even speak with me.

Another approach was withdrawal—simply no contact. Unsure of what to say or how to act, they kept quiet and went on with their lives. I don't think there was an intent to hurt, but there was hurt.

Fortunately for me, some in my community displayed God's love and made a choice to stay involved. To each of them I remain eternally grateful. I was encouraged by their kind words and loving deeds. While I continued to remain attached to the world and its pleasures, this community prayed for me—for my restoration with God, my wife, and my family. They also came alongside and took care of my family—something I'm ashamed to admit I had refused to do. In my mind, I had justifiable reasons for the neglect: My selfish needs and happiness were most important.

Their support for my wife and family was incredible. Several of our closest friends (I was off creating my new circle of secular friends) stepped in and loved my family in tangible ways. They stayed close to them, providing support in every way, even financially when needed. They played with my children and took them places that I should have been taking them. Close friends provided the core Christian values and role modeling for them. Their encouragement helped my wife stay strong in the Lord and to seek Him even in the darkest of times. This community stepped in and became Christ to my family.

While I was clearly out of God's will and not very lovable, they continued to pray for me and love me. I didn't realize just how unrelenting my community was. Several men continued to reach out to me. They didn't condone my actions but in love pursued me, keeping the doors open for restoration and fellowship.

PAINFUL REBUILDING

After more than eighteen months, God began to answer their prayers. My job required me to move more than six hundred miles away. The divorce was moving forward, and we were at the point of dividing our assets. All of a sudden I felt shaken, alone, and aware of all I was about to lose. God was working from within, and my community was working all around me.

Quietly God began to open the eyes of my heart. I allowed the Spirit of God to regain control of my life. I couldn't believe that anyone would open his or her arms and embrace me. I was ashamed and embarrassed. I knew I was wrong and sought God's forgiveness. He was faithful and put His loving arms around me. I went to my wife and asked her if she could find forgiveness in her heart. I wanted to begin rebuilding our lives.

The rebuilding has been painful for both of us. We still have issues to work on, but I've learned to stay engaged and seek answers to our questions. Our love is stronger and deeper than ever before.

I'll be eternally indebted to my wife for remaining faithful to God and for allowing me back into her life. And I'll be eternally grateful for a community that displayed God's love and grace—love and grace that wasn't just verbally communicated but lived out in my life.

God has been faithful beyond my understanding. I've been restored in relationship to Him. I've finally come to understand and experience His love more deeply. God used this time to answer many of the quiet yet nagging questions deep within my soul. For the questions that are still unanswered, He has given me a heart committed to pursuing the answers through His Word and through the community of friends He has blessed me with.

In recent years, I've reflected on my community and how my decisions impacted those closest to me. I was blessed with a significant community, but wasn't aware of my own responsibility to them to not walk away from tough issues but to stay engaged and address them. So often I was the one reaching out to help others, but I was unable to ask for help for myself.

TURNED AROUND

God has used my journey to teach not only me but also those within my restored community. My wife and I have both had the opportunity to share our story with others. We've been privileged to share in others' lives and to open our hearts, offering words of hope and encouragement. What a great God we have! He took my evil heart and selfish actions and turned them around to use for His glory.

What can you learn about community from my journey? First, we all need community. Whether large or small, we all must have community. Learn to recognize your community and nurture it. Ask God to reveal Himself to you and to reveal to you each person whom He would have be a part of your community.

Second, you'll find several levels to your community, much like a series of concentric circles—starting from the inside with some very close and intimate friends and working out toward the more casual acquaintances. It has taken many years to build the relationships we now have with our closest friends. We've laughed in the good times and cried in some difficult ones. To this day we're still growing and learning together.

Third, a key component of community is accountability. I've asked several men in my life to hold me accountable for my actions and to hold me true to my word. Each one has permission to ask any questions of me, at any time. When I travel, I stay in touch with them. At their request, I do the same in their lives.

This is my story. I hope that sharing a little of my journey will be an encouragement to you. My hope is that it will help you recognize your community.

Embrace your community. Maintain your friendships. Most important, seek God and keep Him at the center of your life. May God bless you and keep you.

17

A Story of Faithfulness

I've saved the best story for last. It's the story of my wife, Suzi. She has lived all of her adult life in that hard and indefinable world of being a pastor's wife. Perhaps I'm biased, but there's no more difficult environment in which to live. Her words about community go far beyond the boundaries of being a pastor's wife, however.

———=⊰○⊱=———

J immy and I have had some rousing discussions about everything from why our favorite football team struggles to have a winning season to deep issues facing our church. And we've spent hours together talking about community.

You'd think that after worshiping in one place for twenty-seven years, I would have community down pat. Surely after years of being a part of small groups, ladies' Bible studies, and choir I would at least be able to give a definition of community. I find that I cannot! But I also know that I'm not alone in struggling to explain clearly the concept of community.

Perhaps the problem is that we're trying to define a concept that's indefinable. It's like love. Is there ever a time when we can say with great surety, "This is the total definition of love"? I don't know about you, but just when I feel certain about what community is and how it feels to be a part of one, something happens within my community that changes its borders.

But however much I wrestle with the definition, I do know this: I can't do without community, just as I can't do without love.

CARRIERS OF CHRIST

Being in one place for twenty-seven years has been an extraordinary privilege, one that has allowed me to be a part of various communities. As a young mother, what often kept me sane was being able to laugh and cry with other young moms. Those days were made even richer when a woman with a lifetime of wisdom would come close and whisper words of encouragement that gave us perspective and hope. In those days, community meant an empathetic ear and the voice of truth. I needed both...I still do.

C. S. Lewis said, "God works in us in all sorts of ways. But above all, He works on us through each other. Men are mirrors, or carriers of Christ to other men. Usually it is those who know Him that bring Him to others. That's why the Church, the whole body of Christians showing Him to one another, is so important." Those from our church who have invited me to experience community have been the mirrors of Christ in my life. Their offers of friendship and their desire to connect their hearts to mine have touched the part of my soul that was designed for fellowship.

I've also been through dark nights of my soul when others in our community of believers have carried Christ to me. In 1997, our world came to a grinding halt when I received the news that I had breast cancer. As the report began to spread throughout our church, I was overwhelmed with calls, letters, cards, and visits. I honestly don't think all the folks responded simply because I was the pastor's wife.

What made them react as they did? I sincerely believe their actions were the result of a firm belief that the church is the living body of Christ. My illness became their illness. And I've seen that scenario repeated hundreds of times over the years.

Several years ago our small group decided that instead of doing a Bible study, we would give each person an opportunity to tell their story. At the conclusion of each story, the rest of us were to describe for the speaker a picture of how God might see them. It sounded like a great idea…but I wasn't going first!

An amazing thing happened after everyone shared. Each story made its way into my heart and left an indelible mark. The stories buzzed around in my head for days. I hadn't expected that. I thought the telling would be cathartic for the teller—I had no idea how being a listener would transform me. Each of us is so different, yet all of us have the same core desire for someone to listen to the story of our journey—the good, the bad, and the ugly—and still not walk away.

Even in Disappointments

In a world where our pictures of ourselves are so distorted, it's such a relief to come to church and have a handful of people love me and tell me the truth. Have you experienced the thrill in your heart of someone's enjoying the best parts of you but also knowing the worst—and still cheering for you? That's community.

I would be less than honest if I didn't tell you there have been times when my desire for connection was rebuffed or a sense of belonging to a community was absent. There's a longing in my soul for more community than I've already experienced. I've tasted the appetizer…now I want dinner. The irony of my desire is born out of a wider awareness: First, perfect community will never be realized here on earth. Second, even when I'm in the midst of a wonderful community, I'll be disappointed at times, and I'll disappoint my community as well.

And that's where it gets good! As Tim Hansel puts it in his book *Holy Sweat,* "Watching our fumbling, faltering humanity, God says, 'Yes, this is the way I want to continue to express my incarnation to the world.'" God wants the world to watch us commune with one another, even in our disappointments, and He wants to give them a living tableau of what fellowship with Him resembles. And like the illustration of our life being an unfinished tapestry with loose, chaotic threads on the one side—we know God is weaving a beautiful finished tapestry on the other. As He weaves with people and events in hand, I believe He uses community to participate in His design.

With all its imperfections, community is the place where I grow. It's worth the risks. One simple word of encouragement at Bible study becomes a golden thread of truth. Walking with a dear friend who has suffered repeated loss and survived is the strong red thread of hope. And being urged to stay on the path when the way is rough is the brilliant white thread of faith.

A tapestry without color is indecipherable. A Christian without community is incomplete. Admittedly, we're a motley crew—this church with the funny name. But my life would be a colorless, indecipherable, incomplete picture without others reflecting the image of God.

My Prayer for the Church

I'm sitting in my study, at home. I'm all alone. I have the house to myself—except for our dog, Lucky, who's asleep in my chair. I've just realized: It's done. The book is done. What I wanted to say about community has been said—at least for now.

It's a weird feeling. For so many months I've spent my time capturing thoughts and creating ideas. So many nights as I was about to fall asleep, I would quickly grab the notepad by our bed to jot down something that came to mind. I remember more than once pulling my car onto a side street and scribbling a story on a scrap of paper; I feared it would disappear from memory as quickly as it came. My study at home and my office at church will no longer be littered with dozens of legal pads, filled with barely legible words. (I write best longhand—no computer for me.) A project that began a couple of years ago as little more than a dream is finished.

Well, almost finished.

I have one more thought; actually it's a prayer. It's my prayer for Church at Charlotte. No, let me be bold. It's my prayer for *your* church as well. So many good things are happening at our church. Community is being found by so many and in so many ways. But I want more.

My prayer for our church and for yours draws its energy and shape from a prayer in the Bible. It's Paul's prayer for the church at Ephesus:

> I pray that out of his glorious riches he may strengthen you
> with power through his Spirit in your inner being, so that
> Christ may dwell in your hearts through faith. And I pray
> that you, being rooted and established in love, may have
> power, together with all the saints, to grasp how wide and
> long and high and deep is the love of Christ, and to know
> this love that surpasses knowledge—that you may be filled
> to the measure of all the fullness of God.[1]

It's a great new-covenant prayer. Paul prayed for the Ephesian believers (and for us) with an awareness of God's riches that we possess because of Christ. He was thrilled with the knowledge that we're empowered by the Holy Spirit so that the Father's purpose can be realized in our lives. Then came the focus—the love of Christ. He longed that we might know and experience Christ's love to the point that it fills our very being. What a wonderful, powerful prayer!

Drawing from these great realities, here's my prayer for the church:

> Father,
>
> My prayer today is for the church. It's a prayer of vision, of
> what isn't now but could be. I know You love the church;
> Father, I do too. I pray that You will release Church at

Charlotte to be a community that reflects Your Son, Jesus. I pray that we will be a loving community.

I pray that elders' meetings will be more about worship and shepherding and less about business.

I pray that facades will be replaced by honest struggle.

I pray that self-centered attitudes of "What's in it for me?" will give way to attitudes of serving others.

I pray that the Scriptures not only will be studied but will stir a passion in us to know You more.

I pray that judgment of others will be overshadowed by radical grace given to all.

I pray that the unbelieving world will see a loving group of people living out their faith and be unable to explain it away in human terms.

I pray for community to become contagious and spread to everyone in our church.

Thank You, Father, for loving me, for speaking to me through Your Son, and for giving me Your Holy Spirit to make this supernatural life possible.

I pray all this in the powerful name of the One whose shed blood provides forgiveness and established the new covenant—the name of Jesus.

Amen

Notes

INTRODUCTION

1. Hebrews 12:12.
2. Hebrews 1:2.
3. This quote from Dietrich Bonhoeffer is drawn from George
   H. Guthrie, *Hebrews* in *The NIV Application Commentary Series*
   (Grand Rapids: Zondervan, 1998), 182, quoting Mary Bosanquet,
   The Life and Death of Dietrich Bonhoeffer (New York: Harper and
   Row, 1968), 277-8.

CHAPTER ONE

1. Ecclesiastes 1:2.
2. 2 Corinthians 3:4-6.
3. Ray Stedman, *Authentic Christianity* (Portland, Oreg.: Multnomah,
   1975), 39-40.

CHAPTER TWO

1. Galatians 3:1-3,5.
2. Hebrews 10:19-25.
3. Ezekiel 36:25-26,28.
4. See Dwight Edwards, *Revolution Within* (Colorado Springs: Water-
   Brook, 2001), for a fuller discussion of these four provisions of the
   new covenant.

5. Ezekiel 36:26; Hebrews 10:22; see Hebrews 10:16.
6. Hebrews 7:22.

CHAPTER THREE

1. Genesis 1:26.
2. Jeff Imbach, *The River Within* (Colorado Springs: NavPress, 1998), 210.
3. Hebrews 10:24-25.
4. Exodus 3:7-8.
5. Ezekiel 34:11-12.
6. John 1:14, NASB.
7. John 1:14, MSG.
8. James Houston, "Make Disciples, Not Converts," *Christianity Today,* October 1999, 28.

CHAPTER FOUR

1. Philip Yancey, *What's So Amazing About Grace?* (Grand Rapids: Zondervan, 1997), 70.
2. Zephaniah 3:17.

CHAPTER FIVE

1. Proverbs 29:18, KJV.
2. Esther 4:14, KJV.
3. Galatians 4:19.
4. Colossians 1:28-29.
5. Colossians 2:2-3.

CHAPTER SIX

1. Ephesians 1:17, NLT.

CHAPTER SEVEN

1. Dwight Edwards, *Revolution Within* (Colorado Springs: Water-Brook, 2001), 131.
2. Ezekiel 36:27.
3. Romans 7:6.
4. 2 Corinthians 3:6.
5. John 7:38-39.
6. David Wilkerson, *The New Covenant Unveiled* (Lindale, Tex.: Wilkerson Trust, 2000), 6.
7. Henri J. Nouwen, *The Way of the Heart* (New York: Ballantine, 1981), 15.
8. Galatians 3:3.
9. Matthew 5:3.
10. Penelope J. Stokes, *Beside a Quiet Stream* (Nashville: J. Countryman, 1999), 130.
11. Jeff Imbach, *The River Within* (Colorado Springs: NavPress, 1998), 42.

CHAPTER EIGHT

1. Hebrews 10:24-25.
2. Job 6:14-15.
3. Proverbs 17:9.
4. 1 Peter 4:8.

5. 1 Corinthians 13:3, MSG.

6. See Larry Crabb, *Shattered Dreams* (Colorado Springs: WaterBrook, 2001), for a more complete treatment of this subject.

7. Matthew 9:11-12.

8. 2 Peter 1:3.

CHAPTER NINE

1. 2 Corinthians 4:7.

2. 2 Corinthians 4:7.

3. The following verses, paraphrased, with emphasis added: 2 Corinthians 3:4; 3:5; 3:12; 2:14.

CHAPTER TEN

1. Mark 10:43-44.

2. 2 Corinthians 5:18.

3. Ray Stedman, *Authentic Christianity* (Portland, Oreg.: Multnomah, 1975), 163.

4. 2 Corinthians 6:11-12.

5. 2 Corinthians 3:17.

6. 2 Corinthians 3:18.

7. 1 Corinthians 10:31.

8. Isaiah 43:6-7.

9. Michael Card, *A Violent Grace* (Sisters, Oreg.: Multnomah, 2000), 146.

10. Colossians 1:27.

CHAPTER ELEVEN

1. Ephesians 4:2.
2. Philippians 2:3.
3. Colossians 3:12.
4. Titus 3:1-2.
5. Micah 6:8.
6. Isaiah 31:1.
7. Spiro Zodhiates, ed., *The Complete Word Study Dictionary: New Testament,* rev. ed. (Chattanooga, Tenn.: AMG, 1993), 1482.
8. Zodhiates, *Study Dictionary,* 1208.
9. James 4:10.
10. Proverbs 11:2.

CHAPTER TWELVE

1. Psalm 28:1,7-8.
2. 1 Corinthians 1:27.
3. 2 Corinthians 12:9.
4. Dallas Willard, *The Divine Conspiracy* (San Francisco: HarperSanFrancisco, 1998), 27.
5. Gordon T. Smith, *Courage and Calling* (Downers Grove, Ill.: InterVarsity, 1999), 125.
6. 1 Corinthians 12:7.
7. Romans 12:6.
8. Ephesians 4:12-13.
9. 1 Corinthians 12:18.

CHAPTER THIRTEEN

1. John 13:34-35.
2. Hebrews 10:25.
3. Hebrews 12:2.
4. See Hebrews 12:3.
5. 1 Peter 2:11.
6. Charles Swindoll, *Intimacy with the Almighty* (Nashville: J. Countryman, 1999), 8.
7. 1 John 4:12.
8. See 2 Corinthians 5:14.
9. Gary M. Burge, *The Letters of John* in *The NIV Application Commentary Series* (Grand Rapids: Zondervan, 1996), 196-7.
10. 1 John 4:11.

CHAPTER FOURTEEN

1. See 1 Peter 4:8.

EPILOGUE

1. Ephesians 3:16-19.

Acknowledgments

God has used many people throughout the process of writing this book. My family, friends, and coworkers have been in the stands cheering me on. When I wrestled with my thoughts, they prayed. And when the book was finally finished, they rejoiced.

My deep thanks to Church at Charlotte, especially to those who have been with me since the beginning. You allowed me, at twenty-eight years old, to have the awesome privilege of becoming your pastor. Through the years we've spent together, you've been and continue to be my community.

No pastor can lead a church without the support of his staff. And although I'm terribly biased, a finer staff couldn't be found. Each time one of you stopped in my office to offer a word of encouragement, you strengthened me to keep on keeping on. Thank you.

To the elders, who have shared my passion for community: Thank you for giving me the time to write and for allowing it to be a priority for the last year.

To my three men's groups: You are community in the flesh! To the Wednesday group: You've given me a place to be one of the guys. Thank you for your willingness to be transparent and for making our meetings a safe place for me to share my heart. To the Thursday crew: You'll never know how many times I held that "writer's block" in my hands and smiled. Thank you for praying. And to the Friday gathering: Community is being birthed among us. Thanks for your commitment to the group.

To the many friends who have shared the journey with me: Your love and consistent support gave me the confidence to flesh out my passion and to stay on task. Larry and Rachel, how many hundreds of conversations have we had together? You were the first ones to believe I had a message worth telling. You've shared your hearts, time, and expertise with me. May the journey continue.

Jeff and Nancy, we've experienced so much of life together. You've been an enduring example of community that doesn't walk away—ever. "Thank you" just doesn't seem to cover it, but my deep thanks just the same.

Mark and Terri, thanks for always loving me enough to give it to me straight. Mark, you willingly took on additional burdens at the office so I could have time to write. And while I was on sabbatical, you filled the pulpit with excellence.

Bob and Nancy, you've been incredible examples of community in action. Your home is usually filled with guests because you so effortlessly and generously care for others. Thank you for caring for me and my family many, many times.

Walt and Patti, you came into my life more than thirty-five years ago. And since that time your faithfulness to the Lord has challenged me to walk the talk. If I were to make a list of the people who have influenced my spiritual development significantly, your names would be there.

Mark and Norma, Dave and Terri, Palmer and Lynne, I'm a "wealthy" man because of friends like you.

Two faithful women have worked long hours typing, reading, editing, and retyping my manuscript...without complaint! Judi and Karen, you both have gone above and beyond the call of duty. My heartfelt appreciation for all you do.

I'm also grateful for the new friends I've made during this process. Thank you, Thomas Womack, for taking my thoughts and making sense of them. Thanks to Laura Barker, Don Pape, and the folks at WaterBrook for giving me this wonderful opportunity.

To Sealy and Curtis Yates, even though you're Angel fans (go Yankees!), you've helped guide me through the world of publishing. You do what you do so well. Thank you.

Mom and Dad, our home was a place where you nurtured and supported all my dreams. You still do. Thank you for your love and for being godly role models. Thanks also to Tim and Christi, Beth and Bruce for living out community in our family.

Finally, my deepest thanks to four incredible women. To my three beautiful daughters—Kelly, Jackie, and Graylyn—your love and smiles give me courage every day. No father could be prouder. And to my biggest fan, my amazing wife, Suzi. Thanks for pointing me to Christ, for walking by my side, and for loving me. I love you.

To learn more about WaterBrook Press and view
our catalog of products, log on to our Web site:
www.waterbrookpress.com

WATERBROOK
PRESS